The

Happiness

Handbook

A Practical Guide to

Transforming your Life

Clearing up the Past
Living in the Present
Creating your Future

Landon Carter

THE HAPPINESS HANDBOOK
A practical guide to transforming your life Published by Marshall and
McClintic Publishing Nevada City, CA 95959
Text copyright © 2023 Landon Carter

Landon Carter's back cover photo by Carrie Dobbs,
Takaka, New Zealand
Cover artwork by Susan R. Whiting
Font- Times New Roman
Layout by Margie Baxley
Printed in the United States of America First Edition , July 2023
ISBN: 978-0-9910446-8-9

Contents

PROLOGUE

Have you ever wished you had the handbook for how to be a happy human being on planet earth? I know I have, especially when things just didn't seem to be working and I didn't know what to do about it. I intend that this book is just what you have been looking for – a "how to," guide for having your life be filled with love, happiness, contentment, and a sense of well-being.

I won't be suggesting how to control the circumstances of your life (lots of books do that), but rather how to deal with the circumstances that arise. So that you feel confident that you can handle whatever challenges life brings and remain in a relatively happy state.

Some people talk about "empowerment," as if you lacked some ill-defined power that was keeping you from creating what you want and realizing your full potential. It may be difficult to believe given some of life's painful experiences you may have experienced, but <u>you are already a powerful creative force</u>. Lack of power is not the issue. It is just that you are creating your reality both internally and externally through a flawed structure dedicated to survival rather than happiness, and you are unconscious about it. To correct this, we will go through a process together of three steps.

Step One: We will bring consciousness to that which is unconscious.

Step Two: You will give up the flawed structure with its patterns of thoughts and behaviors to create space for….

Step Three: Creating new ways of "Being in the World," which will create New Realities.

I have explored many teachings in my 50+ years since starting to "wake up," and found some useful and many not so useful. In this book I have included only those that have made a difference in my life and the lives of those I have trained and coached.

This is one path to the experience of completeness, freedom, and happiness, I believe we all desire. It does not require you to believe in any particular notion or take what I say as the "truth." If you will do the work as we go along together, I think you will be able to validate what you are learning in your own personal experience, and this will make all the difference in your life. So, let's get started.

All the best and welcome to the journey.

INTRODUCTION

It's 1971, I'm 28 years old, living my dream life in Aspen, Colorado, and I am deeply unhappy. How could this have happened? I am the guy who had done everything right, gone to some of the best schools in America, Phillips Academy Andover, Yale, and Harvard Business School.

I had achieved success; three varsity sports, captain of the Yale Ski Team, and captain of the undefeated Harvard Business School Rugby Side. I had been in the Peace Corps in Peru and taught at Escuela Superior de Administracion de Negocios (ESAN), the graduate business school in Lima.

I was working in my ideal job, real estate development of Snowmass-at-Aspen, skiing on my lunch hour, and winning races in motocross during the summer. I thought I was definitely following the path to "happily ever after." Yes, I had already failed at my first marriage, but that was all behind me and I had a new girlfriend.

It looked like I had it all, yet, I thought, "If I had twice or three times as much money, or another condominium on the ski slopes, or more, better or even different stuff by the time I was 40, how will I be happy then, if I am not happy now?" There was a song by Peggy Lee, "Is That All There Is," which resonated with me and I could say it "woke me up," or at least started my process of awakening.

I went to see a local therapist who didn't seem to have the answers and smoking dope didn't solve my problem either. Then I read Paramahansa Yogananda's book, *Autobiography of a Yogi*, as he had already passed on, I realized I wasn't going to get any help there. However, Yogananda's book sparked some deep desire to answer the big questions like, "Who am I really and how can I be satisfied and happy?"

The next book I read was Satya Sai Baba's translated discourses and the words just seemed to jump off the page, as if I was being called. Shortly after that, I set out for India to see what this enlightenment stuff was all about. I remember thinking, "If someone told me 2000 years ago that there was a guy, named Jesus, performing miracles over the hill somewhere in Palestine, and I was a Roman soldier, would I have stayed at the bar for another drink or gone over the hill to see for myself."

As I prepared to leave for India the conversation with my mother did not go well. "I am unhappy and I am going to India to sit in a cave, for as long as it takes, if I have to." My mother tried to convince me not to go and was crying as she said, "What about all that expensive education?" Another part of the story is that she became a devotee of Sai Baba after visiting him while I was in India. So, who knows how things will turn out!

Being with Satya Sai Baba changed my life. Not necessarily because I got all the important questions answered and certainly not because I was instantly enlightened but it showed me, for the first time, that there was at least one other reality and that perhaps the reality I had been living in had some false promises for happiness, deep satisfaction, and fulfillment. It started me firmly on the path of self-inquiry and exploration into the nature of reality.

In June 1972, when I returned to the United States after eight months in India, I took the est Training from Werner Erhard, joined the est staff in January 1973 and began my career as a trainer in the human potential movement. Erhard Seminars Training (est) was one of the training programs popular in the 70s and later became Landmark Education, which still exists and has a very good basic transformational program.

I write all this at the beginning of this Happiness Handbook, to encourage you to look into your own life as I share mine. I certainly had most of the symbols of success for a 28-year-old and could have easily glossed over the underlying emotions and followed the normal corporate path I was headed on, but something deep in me cried out that this life I was leading couldn't possibly be my dream future. While I didn't know it at the time, there was much to discover in the process of me going from "this isn't it" to "this is it." This book is my sharing of what I have discovered and found valuable in my life with the intention that it contributes to you having the life of your dreams.

So, to start your process it is essential that you take an honest look into your own life. Is it possible that you are not as happy as you pretend to be? Are you putting on the good face? Or perhaps, like me, you may have started to see the emptiness of accumulating all that stuff, some of which sits in storage.

You may have topped out like I did, recognizing that achievements and accomplishments don't inherently make you happy and fulfilled. Or you might come from the other end of the spectrum, of feeling you are bottoming out. You are depressed about your current situation, or anxious about the future. You feel defeated or hopeless, as nothing you have tried seems to have worked in giving you a sustained experience of happiness and fulfillment.

Or you might have an OK life by most standards and realize that there is more to life than you are experiencing, something like "this can't be all that life offers."

A moment of reflection. I invite you to take a moment and reflect on your actual overall experience of life, the good and the bad, what you are grateful for and what clearly doesn't work, where you are happy and where you are not, as it is never just one experience covering all areas of our lives. This will be a good starting place as our journey together unfolds. And as you will see, we will be working a lot to clear up those aspects that produce the experience of unhappiness. In essence, eliminating what is blocking your natural ability to be happy. More on this later.

Almost all of those experiences you identified in your own life are a function of living in accordance with the precepts of our "normal reality," what most people would say, "Well this is just the way it is." As we explore this more deeply, you will find that your experience is mostly just the "normal," human condition. It is not your fault that you have gotten to where you are. The experience of unhappiness and various degrees of suffering are the natural by-product of living in this unconscious reality, which is the world as we know it.

My path has been to inquire into how things actually work – at least discovering one version that is not the norm I grew up believing and taking for granted. Step by step, I have been working to bring consciousness, insight and understanding to that which was unconscious to me before.

It has often been said that "the truth shall set you free." But the problem is, we mostly can't see the truth, so we operate out of false premises and assumptions, hoping that with a little more effort we will be happy.

There is a light at the end of the tunnel. However, you first have to see what is true and what is false about the beliefs, assumptions, and premises that make up how you experience your life and what you are sure is just the "way it is."

As with most things in life, you have to know how things actually work to be able to sort them out or fix them. It is kind of like driving your car through life steering by holding onto the rear-view mirror (a metaphor for how your past adversely influences your current reality) and wondering why you keep having crashes. Then finally being able to put your hands on the steering wheel and operate from what is actually happening. Part of this Handbook is the exploration of the false premises and limiting beliefs of the "Illusionary Bubble Reality," we inhabit.

Sai Baba once told me, "The only difference between you and me is that I know who I am, and you don't." It has been my 50-year journey to discover and experience the answer to this question, "Who am I?" And with it, having to face up to how I have been sabotaging my own happiness by operating unconsciously, as if I knew it all. There are two quotes from Carl Jung, father of analytical psychology, who points to where we are going. *"One does not become enlightened by imagining figures of light, but by making the darkness conscious... Until you make the unconscious conscious, it will direct your life and you will call it fate."*

When I was a transformational trainer in the 70's, I used to challenge the participants at the start of each training with this question: "Can you afford the arrogance of living your life as if there is nothing you don't know, the knowing of which would totally transform your life?" This is a good question to ask yourself and really think about.

As we start this journey together, it is necessary that you maintain an open mind, a beginner's mind, to the possibility of discovery. It doesn't mean that you negate what you know, rather that you are willing to question and challenge your most dearly held beliefs and ideas about who you are and the world you inhabit.

If you take the time to do the work of self-inquiry which is what this handbook will lead you through, you will have "aha," moments that give you the sense of finally knowing who you are and how things work. The good thing about what I am teaching is that I am not asking you to believe what I say as if it is "the

Truth," with a capital "T," even though some of what I will teach has been reiterated over the ages by great teachers like Buddha, Lao Tzu, and Christ.

I only ask that you try on certain ideas, like trying on a new suit to see if it fits. Do the ideas fit your personal experiences? Whatever becomes true for you will be validated in your own experience. It will be your wisdom, not just more information. Then, you will be "walking the talk," rather than just having some more information and only "talking the talk."

I wish I had the wisdom of this handbook earlier in my life. I think I would have learned my life lessons earlier and not suffered quite as much, or caused the suffering in others by operating so unconsciously and unknowingly. This is my gift to you, with the intention that you are able to create a life of happiness, successful relationships and the fulfillment of your unique human expression.

I will take you through a step-by-step process in this journey of discovery. We will put together some of the pieces you already know and fill in the blanks to form a workable model for achieving happiness.

This work takes a commitment and it helps to have some idea of where you are going in the beginning before you start. For me the goal has always been enlightenment and becoming the most evolved version of myself I could be. You, I am sure, have your own version of where you want to get to. Of course, "I just want to be happy," will do.

Here are some truths I have found that work for me and for many of the people I have had the privilege of interacting with as a trainer and coach. I am not asking you to agree or disagree with these assertions, just take them in as a preview of what you may discover as we go through this process together.

With practice, you can become competent in being the conscious creator of your own transformed life. This is my promise to you.

Where We Are Going

1. Whatever you are experiencing, what is called "living" which is distinguished from what is known as, "your life," (which is your history through time), is always happening in some moment of Now. That means that the experiences we desire, like happiness, joy, peace, and love, must always be available in every moment of Now.

2. Who you truly are is already what you yearn to become: happy, fulfilled, whole and complete, peaceful and joyous. You are not broken and flawed, needing to be fixed. The trick is to let go of what is blocking those experiences. This will be addressed in Chapter 6, Clearing up the Past.

3. You are already a powerful reality creator, creating your reality and everything you experience. You are just doing the creation through a flawed structure, dedicated to survival, rather than happiness. You will realize you have been repeating conditioned patterns of behavior that never produced happiness or love in the first place and to complete the picture, operating within limiting beliefs that don't allow for happiness, success or real love. This will be your area of greatest learning, as you discover how you are already creating your life the way it is. It will take courage to face up to these "truths."

4. Life is not a place or phenomenon to get to, like I am finally enlightened and have arrived, it is a journey of on-going transformation. You will have the tools and techniques necessary to live a transformed and happier life, by the end of this book. You can become more and more proficient in the transformational process through practice.

How To Get the Most from this Handbook

There are two ways to hold information. One is as knowledge, kind of like what you learned in history class, dates you remembered, names and events you memorized for the test. This method may be intellectually stimulating, interesting and even useful in life. However, I doubt it is life changing, and that is what we are up to together–a life changing transformation.

By going through this material, you will certainly learn some things, confirm some things you already know, see how things fit together as a whole, and perhaps be able to see and do things differently as a result. Those are all good and allow you to gain an understanding of this material intellectually.

However, if you are like I was at school: good on the tests and then forgetting most of what I had learned over a relatively short period of time, you know the incompleteness of this type of learning. It is one thing to understand something, it is another to be able to live it.

A metaphor. Over the past 30 years I have trained for and become a world champion masters rower, winning many regattas around the world in single sculls and multiple person boats. However, long before I was truly proficient and able to embody the rowing stroke, I knew and understood how it was supposed to be and could talk a good talk on rowing. Being able to "walk the talk," so to speak, having the stroke embodied so that is just the way I row, took much longer and lots of practice.

For this to be truly useful, you will have to learn

this material experientially. That means taking each concept and finding an experiential example or current experience from your own life that confirms and validates the concept. Only in this way will this process be transformational and make the kind of difference in your life that you aspire to.

A suggestion. It might be advantageous to go through this material with a learning buddy. Reading a section, doing the homework of finding examples from your own life and then sharing those examples and your realizations with your buddy. I have found that will expand and deepen your understanding of this material.

Apropos of Carl Jung's quotes, "making the darkness conscious," or "making the unconscious conscious." We are starting a journey, you and I, to bring the light of consciousness to that which has been unconscious and therefore running and ruining our lives. This involves what is often called "shadow work," for it is by illuminating the darkness with the light of consciousness that the door to freedom and happiness is opened.

Wisdom is really an embodied experience playing out in our lives and provides the basis of what we can legitimately share with others. Without this embodied wisdom that enables us to live a transformed life, we are mostly automatons, reactively sleep walking through life and wondering how to make things better.

Or in the worst case, knowing only as information some of the material of transformation and using the information to make ourselves right and others wrong as arrogant "know it all's."

So, you could read each chapter to get the lay of the land and then go back through the material to come up with your own examples. This may entail allowing yourself to experience experiences you have been avoiding or resisting experiencing. I guarantee that there is light at the end of the tunnel, and the only way out is through, and this is sometimes an uncomfortable process.

This is where your own commitment to freedom and happiness plays such an important role. It is often only this thread of commitment which pulls you through some very dark places. The corollary to this is your willingness to tell yourself the absolute truth. To admit your failings and insecurities, rather than pretend they don't exist, in an attempt to feel good about yourself or prove to others that you have it all together.

A recommendation. I suggest you get a dedicated journal or notebook to record your own examples of the material being covered, your insights and what you are learning that is important to you. I strongly encourage you to <u>make this material personal</u>. Doing this will take a lot longer than just reading through the material. The time you take and the work you do will allow this handbook to guide you through the transformational process that will change your life.

Your first assignment. In your journal start the process now by taking a page for each of the several domains or areas of your life. You define your domains so the total includes all aspects of your life. An example:

Body/Health
Intimate Relationships
Family
Career/Education
Finances
Hobbies/Sports
Spiritual
Leisure/Recreation

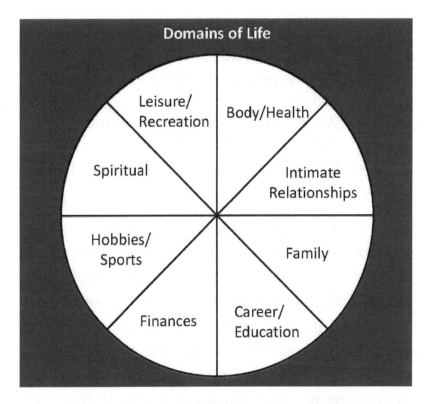

Next, write down a description of your normal experience in each domain. Use a page or more per domain as you will keep adding more insights into how you are showing up as we progress through this learning process. Think about it. It is necessary to know where you are starting in any journey to get to some future goal. This is equally true whether the goal is an internal experience or an external circumstance.

Some Questions

Here are some questions you might ask yourself for each domain:

- How am I showing up in various situations?
- What actions do I take?
- How do others react when I do such and such?
- What is my self-talk about the situation?
- What is my emotional state?
- What is underneath the obvious emotional expressions I am aware of?

For example, you know you get angry at times in your relationship with your spouse. Have you actually looked to see what is under or driving the anger? Perhaps you feel hurt or feel a sense of being invalidated or made to feel inadequate, or a fear of being out of control? Answer what you can at this stage. You will keep coming back to further define your experience in each domain. Just start! That is the action that gets you in the game.

These are the types of questions we will be looking into in this journey of self-inquiry. Once again, I can only point you in the right direction of where to look for your own answers. You have to do the looking and find the answers for yourself. That is the Work.

I can assure you that by exploring these hidden areas within yourself, you will open up to the possibility of more love, happiness, and connection than you thought possible. It is a counter-intuitive, yet miraculous process. My wife, Diane and I have so many examples of clearing up the patterns from our past conditioning that blocked our happiness and loving connection. When we are able to admit to ourselves, talk about and let go of the negative beliefs, behavior patterns, and thought patterns, the result has always been to find we are deeper in love, more connected, happier and more loving and accepting of ourselves and each other. It is the path to freedom and to being able to create the life you desire, and I am eager to share the methods of how you too can have what we have.

So, in many regards, this could be the book you have been looking for, to assist you in finding the answers to the most fundamental questions of what it is to "Be a Human Being," on planet earth.

Everything I share with you is real for me, works for me and for many of the people I have trained and coached over the more than 50 years, since I first began my journey. I didn't make this stuff up, as most of the insights and "aha's," of understanding have been taught by some of the greatest teachers.

I am just someone who has tried to pull together the workable aspects of many disciplines, including psychology, philosophy, spirituality, neuroscience, meditation, etc., to produce this handbook that I wish someone had given me many years ago.

CHAPTER 1

It's All About Your Experience

I have "Happiness," in the title because I think, if we are honest with ourselves, we do virtually everything we do to attain or keep some level of happiness. We may justify our actions or give explanations and excuses in a variety of forms that might appear to be why we do what we do, however I assert, our primary, underlying motivator for action and our intended result of whatever we are up to, is the pursuit of happiness.

This happiness imperative may have many different forms of experience that motivate us: more comfort, less pain, less struggle, more love, less loneliness, more freedom, more self-expression, less submission, less drudgery. And of course, there are the strategies to make you happier: earn more money, go shopping, get a bigger house, eat, drink, smoke to make you fulfilled, satisfied, relaxed or high, have sex, go on a vacation, go to a movie, exercise, lose some weight. I am not saying that any of these things are good or bad, just that the underlining motivation is to be happier. The modus operandi, if expressed might be, "If I do this or accomplish this or avoid that, I will be happy or happier."

Therefore, my premise is that all of us are motivated away from pain and toward happiness, and yet happiness seems to be one of the most difficult experiences to achieve and to sustain. This handbook will explore the many aspects of this illusive experience and provide a proven path to experiencing happiness.

The Categories of Experience

Since this handbook is based on experience, and ultimately your experience, we need to look at what constitutes "your experience." There are only four categories of experience when you actually start to observe what is. This is separate from all the explanations for how things occur like how light photons come into your eyes and end up as impulses in your brain to create an image. Explanations such as the above are basically irrelevant in this handbook, as we actually operate within and from our experience.

The four realms are: thoughts, emotions, body

sensations, and other sensory phenomena (your perceptions). As I discuss each in turn, see if this doesn't include all of what you experience in this and every moment of Now. It may be a shock to you to realize there are only these four categories of experience plus You, the Observer of your experience. Could the Now, this present moment, be that simple?

The Realm of Thought

We often think we are the thinker, thinking thoughts. This is a bit of an Illusion, if you are the thinker, then turn off your thoughts. Don't think for a while. Try it!

If you just attempted to stop thinking, I am sure you failed. The arising of thoughts in your consciousness or awareness is about as automatic as your heart circulating blood in your body and almost as much out of your control. To grasp this idea, stop reading and spend a few minutes just noticing your thoughts. See if you can just notice them drifting by, without getting involved in them. Later we will cover a meditation practice that does just that.

The thought realm includes thoughts, opinions, judgements, and the whole domain of distinctions and naming or labeling of things, like a visual object we see. For example, the thing, a rose, and the word "rose," we instantaneously and automatically connect to the object. We are so entrained to do this; we have a hard time separating the thing itself from its name.

Thought also includes concepts, beliefs and opinions. Concepts like "room, family, I am sick, or my country." Beliefs like the idea or visual concept of anything you are not directly experiencing, such as the "outside world," which becomes a picture in your mind when you are inside your home and not directly experiencing it. Opinions, that the world is unsafe or there is not enough for everyone. As you look deeply into this thought realm, you will realize that these examples are all based on some of your past experiences or concepts you learned which are now in the form of names, images and memories from the past.

Also included are projections into the future which are a combination of mental pictures and images like the memory of the camping trip I went on when I was ten years old and now the expectation of what will happen on our camping trip next week. Or perhaps, the projection of what I fear will happen, based on some traumatic experience from my childhood, when I make my presentation next week at the office.

This is an extensive collection, but you will notice that you can only have one thought at a time, often in quite rapid succession, but still no two thoughts can occupy your mental space at the same time. This law (no two things can occupy the same space in the same unit of time) applies to all things in our Illusionary Reality of which thoughts are perhaps the most ethereal or insubstantial. This is an important observation when we look at being able to focus our attention in the process of creating reality.

As you read through this information about the thought realm and start to relate the material to your own experience, you might start to get a sense of your Observer Self, separate from your thoughts or thinking.

Ask yourself these questions. Who is generating the thoughts? If it is "Me," then who is listening to them? Am I both or neither? Just by hanging out with these sorts of questions you will start to see what is really going on.

Emotions

Emotions include the whole range of emotional energy in its various forms; from hopeless and depressed to joyous and exhilarated. You will notice as you scan your experience of what you call "Me," there is a feeling, an energetic vibration so to speak, and a name you give to the feelings like "fear, anger, or enthusiasm." Also, as you look you will probably see that there is a body sensation, or several body sensations associated with the emotion. If I asked right now as you read this, "Are you angry?" Notice what you do. Did you scan your body to see if there are familiar sensations that indicate to you that you are angry?

We tend to be driven by our emotions, justifying our actions as if the justification or reason we give is the motivator. I disagree with this and if you look, I think you will find that you always (perhaps almost always) are motivated by an emotion or perhaps a painful or uncomfortable body sensation that you do not like. Unhappiness, which is basically an emotion, in all its forms (afraid, sad, depressed, bored, angry, etc.) is the motivator that invariably leads to some behavior in order to correct the situation.

Body Sensations

Body sensations are in the touch realm of the five senses. There is always a location, a shape and size, an intensity, heavy or light, and perhaps a vibrational component to all body sensations. They exist within the limitation of what we identify as our body and are a strong reinforcement of the "I am my mind/body," reality. There is a phenomenon called "phantom limb" which puts the location of the person's experience where the limb used to be, still reinforcing the definition of "myself as a body."

As you scan through your body, you might notice something like "a two-inch band of tightness across my chest," or "a baseball sized ache in my stomach area," or "a pressure above my left eye." You will certainly notice the pressure of your butt on the chair or your feet on the floor as you are reading this book.

If you close your eyes and just follow your sensations around your body, you may notice that not only do they seem to change as you really look at them, but the experience of a whole, complete, integral body is missing.

It is as if, the idea of "my body," is a concept with a variety of physical sensations cobbled together to give credibility to the notion of a solid physical body. Remember, we are looking at your direct experience in this moment of Now and not the apparent solid image of yourself reflected in the mirror.

Other Sensory Phenomena

Smell is in your nose and taste in your mouth. But what about seeing and hearing? This is an important distinction as it ultimately is related to who we truly are, which we will deal with later. If you look at an object - do that - and stay in your experience of seeing, not in your head with the explanations of seeing. I think you will confirm that the experience of "seeing the object," is where the object is, out there in the space in front of you and not in your eyes or brain.

The same can be said about hearing. You hear out in space where you say the sound comes from. This is not to say that the scientific explanations of seeing and hearing aren't useful when talking about glasses or hearing aids. It's just that we operate in a world of experience and need to separate our experience from the realm of explanation, which is part of our experience but, in the form of thoughts. This is not a trivial distinction and should help us in knowing reality as it is.

Remember we are looking at all the elements of your experiential world - experiences in or around your body (like thoughts, emotions, and body sensations) and now outside your body. So, experientially, if you say, "I know that person is real," it is because you have the direct experience of seeing them and perhaps hearing them over where you say they are, as in where they are literally standing. The experience of seeing constitutes the greater part of the bubble reality you inhabit and as we will discuss later has some major potential flaws based on our beliefs, biases, and interpretations. For now, let's just agree that it is one of the categories of experience.

Becoming the Observer of Yourself
The ability to observe is a very useful tool to employ as we progress on this journey of self-inquiry and the

discovery of the nature of reality. Just as you needed to observe your own thoughts, emotions, and body sensations in the previous section to validate what I was describing, you can become the observer of how you are "showing up" in life. It is as if you are seeing the whole play from a position in the audience while at the same time playing one of the roles on stage.

Normally, we operate transparently to ourselves, as if the origin of our experience comes from some place inside our body, behind the eyes perhaps, while we are reacting to and dealing with what is out in front of us. This needs to shift.

To do this work, we need to expand the locus of our experience to several feet behind our head (a useful position to take), or to become the space within which our overall experience of our selves arises and start to "see ourselves in action."

Cultivating this self-awareness will be important as you progress in the self-inquiry outlined in this handbook and will be reinforced when we talk about meditation later.

Summary

You have an experience of observing the four categories of experience and noticing that you were observing your experience and slightly separate from your experience. Yet the sum total of our internal experience is what we normally call "Me." I think this, I am angry, I feel sick, I believe this or that. We always have the "I," attached to the experience.

You wouldn't say, "I am my dress," for "I have this dress." Start to try out similar language with your various experiences. Rather than "I am angry," try out "I have some anger right now." Experiment. See what happens.

CHAPTER 2

The Illusion We Live In

An understanding of the nature of the "Illusion," we live in, what we call "Reality," is a necessary backdrop to the three domains of past, present, and future, which we will focus on. I intend to bring some clarity to this changing Illusionary mist we call "just the way it is."

This could be a bit of a stretch for you, so just stay with me. An analogy would be like trying to talk to fish about water when water defines everything in their life. It is so transparent to them that they never examine it, never question it.

There are some fundamental misperceptions or mistakes in the makeup of the Illusion/Reality that misleads us and prevents us from having the life we desire. Some misperceptions show up in our notions and beliefs about how the world works and for others it is the beliefs about ourselves.

I will go into each of the following distinctions in more detail. First, what are the foundations of this Illusion

1. The Illusion's fundamental essence is "Agreement," (not material particles). The more agreement, the more real things appear.
2. We have misidentified ourselves as a THING in this Illusion/Reality and have forgotten, "Who We Truly Are."
3. Creation occurs from the most etheric (like thoughts) to the most solid (like manifest things). A useful structure we will come back to is: BE > DO > HAVE (RESULTS).
4. The Illusion flows out of Consciousness. The everything/nothing many call God.

Creating the Illusion

The western religious traditions state, "God created the heavens and earth," and "In the beginning was the word," both of which are pointing to the initial process of reality creation. However, most people's interpretation of their version of God and how they see the world comes out of the very Illusionary paradigm we are exploring.

In this dualistic paradigm, God becomes another thing, something outside ourselves that requires various forms of interaction, depending on the historical time and the beliefs of the religion. So, I am going to refer to that divine state or phenomena in secular terms as "Awareness or Consciousness," itself.

The notion of Awareness is something we will return to often in this handbook, as it is experiential and available to all human beings in every moment of Now, regardless of religious belief or any other distinguishing factors. However, the mesmerizing pull of the Illusion keeps us in a trance like state, sleep walking through life until we "Wake Up," and even then, the Illusion keeps pulling us back. That is why this is a handbook of the tools you will need to keep waking up over and over again.

In the normal course of life, Awareness is missed and remains hidden, when in fact it is the most real, most available aspect of our entire experience. This is the biggest mistake we as humans can make, as it disconnects us from the very source of our alive, creative power. We will return to this conversation many times and suggest some practices to allow you to directly experience the reality of your own Consciousness, your True Self.

Be > Do > Have
I am making the case that who you are "Being," has the power to create the experiences you want, love

and happiness. The accomplishments, titles, money and stuff you have in your life are pale symbols of what you really desire. Mostly the Illusion is oriented in the opposite direction to how it actually works. It says go from Have> Do > Be or Do > Have > Be.

An example, suppose you are feeling inadequate and not too good about yourself. Some might label that as "low self-esteem". Now the solution to this in the Illusion looks like, "if I accomplish X or get recognition for Y, then I will feel good about myself". This isn't stated as such of course, it is just assumed. Think about it. "If I Have more money, I will be secure and happy." "If I Have a relationship, I will Be experiencing love." "If I Do this or accomplish that, I will Have those results, get recognized, be admired and then I will Be happy." "If I buy a boat, go boating, then I will be happy."

"If I go on a vacation, I will have fun, I'll be happy. If I go to a movie, I will get out of this boredom and be happier. And after several years in many marriages, if I DO divorce and I no longer HAVE this spouse, I will Be happier. If I buy this or get that, or if I lose weight, etc., I will be happy."

This is a good place to stop reading and to spend a few moments coming up with your own examples of how you have been subconsciously programmed.

An Exercise

Continue to look for examples in your own life, then write them down in your journal. Become a curious observer of your life. Do you pursue happiness through:

- purchases?
- relationships?
- activities?
- achievements?
- stuff, the house, the car, or more, better, different versions of what you already have?

It is important to observe and tell the truth to yourself about <u>how it really is for you.</u>

For me, it was always the excitement of the next project, the next adventure, or the new relationship that provided the happy high I was looking for. Then came the gradual decline as reality set in and eventually I was once again in the resident state of boredom and dissatisfaction.

Exercise

Take some minutes of reflection and self-inquiry to write your examples under the domain they pertain to or just generally as to what your strategy is to achieve happiness. In my experience, I don't know of anyone who doesn't have some degree of "this will make me happy," at least as their unconscious starting position when exploring a domain in their life. It could be in any domain, relationships, health, body, career, etc. I know it is my default position, even though I also know it is a false promise.

This default position, the norm, is inherently flawed because it states that the promise of happiness is in the future, when you Do or Have what you say will bring you happiness. And sometimes it seems to do just that, at least for a short period of time. But this means that in the majority of your life, you are experiencing some form of unhappiness - boredom, upset, stress, disappointment, depression, negative feelings and not happiness.

The overall sense being, "this isn't it; this isn't really what I want my life to be," and looking to future accomplishments or experiences for some relief from the dissatisfaction. From a Buddhist perspective, this defines suffering.

In this scenario, the future is always where salvation is, and the present moment is just a necessary stepping- stone in an endless unhappy journey.

Victim Mentality

If you look more closely, you will see what you do not want to see, that this supposedly causal relationship between the outside circumstance of what you Have or what you Do or what someone says or does, or what is occurring, appears to make you a <u>victim of those circumstances</u>. Whether it is a good experience or a negative one! Your internal experience of Being seems to be at the effect of forces and situations that you have little control over.

Some people say, "I'm not a victim, look at all I take responsibility for doing to create the results in my life." Yes, that is a form of responsibility, that is still operating within the paradigm of the Illusion, so it is a lower form of responsibility. And if it really worked then everyone who has lots of money would be happy and on the negative side, everyone who is criticized would be upset and this of course is not true as many examples demonstrate.

We will come back to this conversation about responsibility because there is a higher order of responsibility; Being 100% responsible for your entire experience and for the life you are living and creating.

One of the major underlying principles of the Illusion, that <u>outside circumstances cause our internal experience</u>, is false. For this reason, I assert that we all "become addicted to **False Cause**." Think of how much you and others have circumstantial reasons for why you feel good, or you bitch, moan, complain, blame, and come up with excuses that always point the finger to someone or something outside yourself.

An example of real cause would be, if it is raining, then everyone who is outside gets wet. Period, end of story. With regard to your internal experience, believing in False Cause is a trap that will ultimately keep you from being responsible for your own experience and your ability to Be Happy.

It may be useful to make a distinction here so that you can review your life properly. I refer to the distinction between something in the outside world that <u>causes</u> your internal experience versus something that <u>triggers</u> a pattern of thoughts, emotions, body sensations, and behaviors.

This distinction is very important because the starting point in the process of clearing things up is always the same - something happens in your outside perceptual experience (like a person saying something or an event happens) or in your body (like an accident – stubbing your toe).

When that event happens, if you wake up, you can pursue a course of action in which you start to clear up the triggered pattern and thereby become less reactive to the trigger in the future. But if you remain asleep (in the trance), you will continue to act out the pattern and reinforce its hold over you.

We will come to a further discussion of this choice in Chapter 6, Clearing up the Past.

Not Your Fault

Before talking about the next building block of the Illusion, I want to talk a bit about how we got into this predicament in the first place. It is not your fault that you believe these things or operate from these premises in living your life. It was just what was available to you when you were born and you were trying to make your way and be accepted in this Illusionary Bubble Reality you found yourself in.

You were born into an already existing conversation, as if Reality was an ongoing play and you had to find a role that would ensure that you would be accepted and fit in. At that point, you really didn't have any choice and you didn't make all this up.

However, once you see the several fallacies of the Illusion, and acknowledge the extent to which they exist in your own life, you will then see the possibility of not being limited by these misperceptions and false beliefs. This is where we are going and we have some work to do first to get there.

Identifying Yourself as a Thing

The next fundamental mistake is Identifying yourself as a Thing, a solid Object, separate from other people and the world around you. We will look at the way to decouple your Self from this rigid and limited identity later in this Handbook. But for now, let's agree that most people's and perhaps your position is, "Yes, of course I am a separate Person with my own unique needs, desires, strengths, and failures. I'm over here and they are over there. How could this not be the way it is?"

Summary

You have looked at how you are addicted to False Cause in your own life and the various strategies you have employed to try to achieve a sense of lasting happiness. You have started to wake up from the trance of unconscious conditioning and are beginning to question if pursuing the outward symbols of success is keeping you from having the life you desire.

CHAPTER 3

Agreement Based Illusionary Reality

To gain a more robust picture, let's bring in the notion that the Illusion, the bubble reality you live in and you as an object in that reality, are fundamentally made up of Agreement. Scientists keep looking for some fundamental particle, yet undiscovered, that will explain reality. They have not found it yet. In our conversation about the Illusion, let's start by looking at these so called "solid objects."

I recommend that you read this slowly. At its core, any object agrees with what is <u>not that object</u>. We have the object "A," and its counterpart, everything that is "not A," including the dimension of space or what most of us call emptiness, which is really defined by a measurement of distance and volume.

To help you think about this, imagine only one color that extends infinitely. Would you notice it? Remember everything is that color including you looking. The answer is "No."

To notice a color requires a contrasting color, like black defines white and vice versa. White speaks to the existence of black. This is the very nature of the <u>dualistic reality</u> we live in. Everything is basically defined by what it is not. They are necessary pairs.

Also, all "Things," are measurable, by weight, length, volume, color, vibration, density. Measurement is an agreement passed down through time and coming from some authority, like PhD scientists today saying what subatomic particles are or the king of yore who said, "mine is now the standard foot!" Of course, the king was only the king by agreement, using force to enforce his power at times, nevertheless, Agreement.

Take a solid object and you will notice that any other solid object agrees with its existence since "no two things can occupy the same space in the same unit of time."
Your body is a more-or-less solid object and of course anything you bump into confirms that.

We know that physicists are challenging the very nature of Reality and we know that there is much more space than anything solid (like neutrons, quarks, etc.) in what we call solid objects.

However, for all of us in this discussion it is best to accept the apparent solidity of the physical universe. This is a healthy perspective and necessary, in the process of creating a happy life.

The Agreement Spectrum

Here are a few examples, in descending order from more to less solid, without claiming this as a definitive list: The most solid are physical objects. The next level might be how most people (lots of agreement) see the physical world. Consider the following two notions that were later disproved by scientific data and discovery: the earth centric view up until Galileo's time and the notion of a flat earth. Today, "scientific materialism," is the Agreement of the way it is. These world views can last for centuries and become the predominant belief of "how the world is."

This brings us to the distinction between <u>interpretation</u> and physical reality. We live within an interpretation of reality (flat earth) and treat it as if it is as real as the physical reality upon which it is based. One of the ways we operate in the Illusion is to collapse the interpretation and the physical reality and treat them as one. Judgements of others fit into this category, like he is mean, or she is beautiful, as do passing opinions like "that is awful," or "that is difficult."

Part of living in ignorance (not being awake) is not realizing the difference between what your mind has added to the physical reality (your interpretation) and the physical reality itself. Therefore, you must always be challenging your own assumptions and beliefs with a question like, "Is this true?"

Next on the descending scale might come things like slavery, which neither St. Paul nor Aristotle argued against or the subjugation of women. To this day the remnants of these views of "how it is," still show up in the racial and gender biases held by many people. We unconsciously, automatically operate out of these views that are part of our programming unless we investigate their influence in our own lives.

A Moment of Reflection

What are your unexamined, unconscious assumptions? As embarrassing as it was for me to admit, I grew up as a white male chauvinist, with an unstated, unexamined assumption that I was slightly better than most others and glad I was a male. Going to all male schools, as Andover and Yale were at the time, only seemed to reinforce that notion.

So, it might be useful to look at your assumptions and deeply suppressed judgements about race, gender, sexuality, religion, nationality, etc. Just by seeing them for what they are will start to give you some insight as to why you operate the way you do and allow for some choice in the future.

As fewer and fewer people hold to the validity of these world views and more and more people challenge the rightness of a view, it becomes less solid and more flexible. As an example, in our supposedly enlightened western world, the women's suffrage movement in the early 1900's allowed women to finally get the right to vote, yet glass ceilings in our society are still prevalent today. It is less solid, yet still present.

So as the agreement loosens, things change and a new agreement takes its place. From slavery, as an example, to full egalitarianism. While the law says equality, the agreement field within which people live, has yet to fully comply.

Next, let's look at how authority establishes agreement. For example, a judge in a court of law, or a jury deciding guilt or innocence of an accused. What about the committee that determines the rules to a game like soccer, with its worldwide federation?

All of these are positions of authority/agreement that carry more weight in determining reality than would be granted to those people as solitary individuals outside their authoritarian roles. This doesn't mean that there are not significant consequences to these agreed upon realities, like a prison or death sentence, or expulsion from the game for months.

Medical schools, in conjunction with the state, decide who can practice medicine. The Department of Motor Vehicles issues a license to drive. Can you see that we live in a sea of agreement and that there are consequences to each level?

A judge and jury can say you die, regardless of whether or not you actually did the agreed upon crime. Or you may just be excluded, ostracized, or rejected, if you do not comply with what the majority agrees is normal and acceptable–as was the case for some kids in your school, remember?

Cultural norms and mores are agreements. Try walking naked down the street when in town. Yet in a different culture it's not a problem. In fact, in some locales you might be asked, "why are you so covered up?"

Today, a woman can get stoned to death for adultery in one culture and understood as not getting her needs met in another. In some cultures, the women decide all aspects of the relationship including who she sleeps with. What is the foundation of all these different realities that make up the grand Illusion? Different agreements and different levels of agreement as to what is right, wrong, good, bad, acceptable, etc.

Just to tie this together with our previous discussion, agreements are a form of belief. They seem to be necessary to give us a sense of constancy and security in an otherwise, changing, chaotic, impermanent world. And the more fear an individual or a group has, the stronger and more ardently defended the belief will be. Thousands of women (many of them healers) were burned as witches because somehow, they were seen as threats to the belief in Christianity. The Inquisition is another example of a forcefully propagated belief of one form of religion.

We will come back to this conversation in each of the three domains, past, present, and future. The Illusion traps you in its web when you don't see it for what it is. Yet, it is essential to understand how it works when learning how to be happy while creating your desired future. For now, a workable mantra might be:

I surrender to what is physical,
and challenge all my beliefs
to see how useful or limiting they might be.

A Way to Look at Your Life

Think of your reality as a series of concentric circles with you in the center and different domains going outward, ranked in terms of importance to you and the extent to which you experience your ability to influence or create how that domain is.

You are in the center with the most control over that domain. You can influence your self-talk, how you hold various aspects of your experience, and how you deal with your body. You possess the ability to get to a place of neutrality and non-reactivity. Your commitment to happiness and ultimately who you are Being in the world all fall within that domain.

Next, comes your intimate relationships. Being this close and vulnerable to another will bring up some of your deepest wounds for healing and can also produce some of your greatest moments of pleasure. Also, you will see that how you show up and how you hold your partner (your beliefs or interpretations) makes a huge difference. In this way, you begin to gather evidence for how you are creating your reality. Children are somewhere near this domain with a different dynamic and equally able to teach you insights into how you are showing up that gets mirrored by them.

Next, might come your family of origin as these people will also be challenging as they bring up (trigger) past conditioned behavior patterns and unconscious beliefs for you to examine.

As you continue outward from the center, you will examine your relationship with your friends, work environment, your finances and wealth, sports, etc. and finally the world at large.

OUR EXPERIENTIAL UNIVERSE

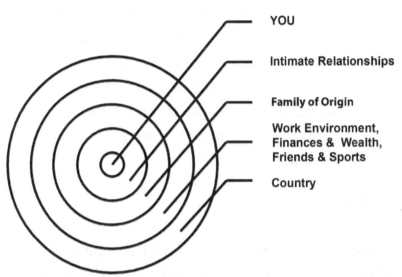

YOU

Intimate Relationships

Family of Origin

Work Environment,
Finances & Wealth,
Friends & Sports

Country

Each concentric circle has degrees of freedom and degrees of control. At the level of the physical universe, it is best to surrender to the way it is - at least as a starting point and a necessary move in order to be happy. Then you can intend a different reality configuration and go about the process of manifesting that reality.

Remember whatever level you are focusing on; it is a function of agreement. With yourself it is only you. With an intimate partner it is just two of you. With your work it may be the entire corporate culture (mores and normative behaviors) that you are dealing with. Within your country, it is a larger, more solid agreement field of what is right, wrong, acceptable, etc.

In the innermost circle, that of your internal experience, you have the most control. This is where the work starts. So, bring consciousness to that which was unconscious and thereby regain your freedom of choice as to how you are showing up. This is always your starting point in the reality creation process; your internal experience, your beliefs, your presentation in the world, who are you Being.

Who Are You?

If you are not a Thing, a solid object existing in this Illusionary Bubble Reality, then who are you really?

Ramana Maharshi, a Hindu holy man who lived in the first half of the twentieth century, attacked this attachment to what he called our "false identity," through this simple question, "Who am I?"

His answer to whatever a student came up with was, "Not that, not that." The goal was to lead the student to the experience of just Conscious Awareness, with no self as form. This is what the Buddhist refer to as Emptiness. When I was with Satya Sai Baba in India in 1972, I had visited Ramana Maharshi's ashram in Tiruvannamalai and learned his simple self-inquiry meditation of asking myself "Who am I?" And following with "Not that, not that," to whatever my mind came up with.

When I returned to Whitefield, outside Bangalore,

I was waiting for Sai Baba to give his afternoon discourse and darshan. I was sitting on the ground next to the aisle, asking myself the question, "Who am I," and Baba walked by me. My eyes were closed, as I was seriously meditating.

Reading my mind he said, "Yes who are you? Ha! Ha! Ha!" I think he just saw the comedy of this illusory life I was enmeshed in and was perhaps telling me not to take myself too seriously. A good lesson.

There is a difference between Who we truly are and who we consider ourselves to be. Looking at "Who we consider ourselves to Be," we have to start with the body, male, female, old, young, etc. All of those definitions are agreed upon in our society.

At a deeper level of agreement, think about how your history is all linked together as memories that have a consistency to them. You didn't jump from one race to another, or one gender to another, except by an agreed upon process.

So, there is a consistency in your story, as one memory agrees with another in describing why and how you are the way you are. Your story makes this separate you an integral part of the overall Illusion as your memories always include a time and place.

All forms exist in this agreement reality, including thoughts which seem perhaps the most ethereal.

They exist for a while and then disappear. Yet, like physical objects only one thought can occupy your thought space at one time.

And isn't your story, your history, nothing more than a loosely connected series of memories (images and thoughts) strung together by you saying, "this too is me," as each one arises separately? You are not the same body you were when you were a child, not one cell! And I doubt that your interests are the same. Certainly, you have changed roles (child to adult, child to parent, etc.)

An Assignment

As you think about the above, let yourself release some of the solidity to the concept of "Who do you consider yourself to Be." Let go of some of your attachment, your identity with this series of memories and your interpretation of who you are. There is a sequential process going on as you read this material. Let yourself experience it.

In your journal, write down all the things, roles, and emotional states you consider yourself to be. Like I am a 79-year-old male, a father, husband, teacher, who is mostly even-keeled and happy. Those are some of my identity features. What are yours?

Once you have your list, then go through the list

asking the question, "Is this really me?" I am only a "father," because I have children and I am not my children - they are what I have and am I what I have? So "father," is just a concept. Am I just a concept? As you go down your list keep questioning, "Am I what I have or what I do (like teach)?" See if you can let go of some of your attachment to each concept of your identity or role you play through observation and reflection.

Your False Self

As the final element in this discussion, let's return to a review of "Who you consider yourself to Be." We have a body, and we are not going to get away from our body in this lifetime. What about your story, your history, your beliefs, even your patterns of behavior based on your upbringing and conditioning?

We will look at these questions and the structure of your False Self in more detail when talking about clearing up the past. However, in terms of the Agreement based Reality, there are people in your life who have parts of your story intermingled with theirs and therefore there is some agreement between you and them as to the story of your past and your identity. The question is who holds you to that identity? Who holds the authority to declare, "this is who I am and this is what I believe?"

I suggest it is you and only you who holds yourself in place, who has been unconsciously living out of an identity which, at best, only partially gives you the experiences you want. Freedom (Moksha in the Hindu tradition) will only come when you start to detach the false identity you have been so attached to from your True Self. This process of detachment is the Path to Freedom.

It is as if you were born into that play I previously described, as an actor, who took on a role and played the role so many times, you forgot you were an actor and thought you were the role itself and the whole play was real. The role became your persona. In Greek, "persona," means "mask," which is what the actors held up in front of their faces when playing a role.

When you can recover your True Self as the actor, to continue the analogy, then you will have freedom of choice, and with choice comes the possibility of new realities.

Bringing Presence to Your Life
Since Living is always NOW, it would seem that our goal should be to bring 100% of our Presence (attention, energy, awareness, consciousness) to this present moment. The process then would be to learn to focus our attention and to strengthen our ability to

be centered in this moment, Being Aware <u>and</u> Being Aware of Being Aware.

The primary method to bring space, freedom and choice to your life will be to clear up your reactive past that seems, too often, to play itself out in the current reality. Think of how much consciousness that would free up.

So, this brings us to two aspects of freeing up consciousness. The first aspect is to build up our mental muscle, our willpower, to Be Aware of Being Aware. This will strengthen your ability to be able to quickly drop the reactivation and eventually to not even be emotionally reactivated.

The second aspect is learning about the nature of "who you consider yourself to be," so you can recognize the reactivation when it occurs, take responsibility for it (own it), let it go, and progress toward loving yourself more fully and making more conscious choices. Then you will be Responding to what is occurring rather than Reacting (important distinction).

Summary
If you have been doing the work of letting go of your hold on your beliefs and your fixed notion of who you are, you might be feeling a little unstable, unsettled, or ungrounded and this can be a bit scary. Letting go

of your attachments, or at least loosening up your grip on your beliefs and idea of who you consider yourself to be, is a necessary part of the process of Self Realization. You are on track. See if you can just let the fear be for now and not do anything in response to it.

CHAPTER 4

Meditation - A Helpful Tool

People define meditation in different ways and there are many different forms of meditation, some of which I have tried over the last 50 years. I have prayed to Hindu gods, focused on a candle, used a mantra, done pranayama until my breath stopped for long periods, and sat for days at a time. A brief story of one of my forays into the practice of Vipassana, (means "to see things as they really are," and is one of India's most ancient techniques of meditation), might be informative at this point.

In my 50s, I attended four 10-day Vipassana retreats over the course of several years. In them, I learned how useless the mind often is, constantly chattering away and demanding my attention as well as how subtle the body sensations are that motivate us – trying to repel discomfort or trying to hold onto or create pleasurable feelings, also how necessary the mind is for getting along in the world.

My first retreat, led by Joseph Goldstein and Sharon Salzberg, of the Insight Meditation Society, used mixed sitting and walking meditations. I took some time to do some training for rowing every day and was able to talk to my roommate in the evenings. By the end, I experienced a kind of "being in the moment," mindfulness which seemed to bring some peace to my life. It prompted me to want more.

After moving to New Zealand in 1998, I attended three retreats at S. N. Goenka's retreat center north of Auckland. These felt like "enlightenment boot camps," on a whole new level.

The rules included not only no talking to or contact with other participants, with instructions to not even look at them or make eye contact. We were to just be with ourselves, night and day.

The first three days, we followed the breath, to increase focus and concentration. Then we moved on to sitting absolutely still and going slowly, in detail, through our bodies, which is the practice of Vipassana. I later called this the agony and the ecstasy experience.

As I sat, I would notice the pains in my body and all the thoughts racing through my mind. Like, "why am I wasting my time, and this is getting me nowhere, and if I just moved a little, I would be more comfortable," or "I wonder if I could build a rowing bike?" which I proceeded to design in detail in my head.

An endless stream of useless, non-productive fantasies and thoughts that constantly took me away from just being present. That was the agony part, hour after hour.

Then, on break, I often experienced the beauty of the natural environment we were in, at a whole new level. Once, I found myself on my knees weeping with joy at how everything was made of light and at the unbelievable pleasure of being alive.

Another time, I felt as if there was a waterfall of pleasurable sensations streaming through my entire body. This was the ecstasy part. No mind, just being alive. Like all experiences, these did not last, as they too were impermanent and couldn't be held onto. Upon leaving one retreat, my brother picked me up, and I was very present and sensitive, I imagined kind of like a newborn baby. We were at a shopping mall and in the food court, I could not handle being around other people, and got lost just going to the men's room. I ended up lying down in the back seat of my brother's car in the parking garage, curled up, and avoiding all the input of our normal world.

I gradually came back to a more normal existence over several days. For some things, the mind and its memory are useful, like not getting lost, and/or perhaps protecting us from too many sensory inputs that would overwhelm us. And of course, the creative imagination is a wonderful ability the mind provides us.

I now hold meditation as a set of practices, just like practicing a sport, with certain intended goals such as maintaining a state of awareness for longer periods of time. I am recommending the following set of practices that have worked for me in the process of transcending my ego nature and becoming less reactive, more responsive, and happier. These practices provide a direct path to experiencing who you are which is Awareness itself.

A Meditation Practice

Set aside a given time for your practice, like 20 minutes, in which you will sit still with nothing else planned. Most teachers recommend sitting upright in a posture that is balanced and attentive, so as to stay present and awake. There is no need to be in a yogic posture that is uncomfortable.

Remember, this is a practice that eventually should translate into everyday life, so you don't need to get too rigid about it. Just set aside the time daily, morning or evening, do the practice and see what happens. Give it about three weeks, <u>then</u> decide if it is working or not, in terms of contributing to your everyday life.

Start with the practice of **focusing your attention** on your breath, which is changing, repetitive, and occurs without you having to make it happen. I suggest following the three-part cycle:

**In-breath, Out-breath,
Then the Pause before the next in-breath**

You can focus on your nostrils, upper lip, abdomen, or lungs; just see how aware you can become. Now many experiences will arise to distract you and in fact even carry you, the observer, away. Memories, plans for the future, random thoughts, emotions, with their accompanying body sensations. The trick is to notice them, without getting engaged in them. They are just part of what you are aware of, like clouds drifting across the sky, while you continue to follow the breath.

At the beginning, it may be too difficult to follow the instructions above. So, begin by counting every breath as you continue to follow it and basically don't engage in the thoughts that arise.

If you find yourself lost in some thought and have forgotten the count, go back to number one again. If you get to 10 in a row, then go back and start again at one. When your mind has settled down a bit and your Observer Presence is stronger, you can drop the counting and just follow the breath. This may take most of the three weeks to be able to settle in, so don't give up. Next, when you get fairly competent in the above practice, you can switch your concentration practice to meditation, to *Being Aware of Being Aware,* (the title of Rupert Spira's book). Start with focusing on the breath, then switch to noticing who or what is aware. This is the heart of meditation, going for the direct experience of who you truly are, Consciousness or Awareness itself.

Instead of the breath, you can substitute physical objects as the point of your focus. Concentrate on really seeing the physical object like a flame of a candle or an object in the room, then switch to who or what is aware of the object.

For example, during one session, you could use your body as the object of your attention. Go through your body from feet to head, slowly, part by part, feeling the body sensations. Notice that you cannot find any solid self in any particular part of the body. Notice there is an Observer Self being aware, then switch to Being Aware of Being Aware of even you observing your experience, like having a thought about a thought.

In another session, have your attention be on the entire space that you are aware of, everything you can see with your eyes wide open. Notice how your awareness is located with each object in the space, your awareness and the objects are co-located, awareness is everywhere, yet it is no thing (nothing, emptiness), located nowhere specific. It is NOW, Here. I recommend that you read that again very slowly.

Who you are is Awareness Being Aware of the objects of your experience, in which your body sensations, emotions, and thoughts, what you call "me," just occur. Being Aware is always in the Present.

Do you see how this practice, if followed in sequence, will lead you closer and closer to bringing Presence to everyday life? Trust me it will.

Here's another example. Imagine you are about to open the door into a meeting in which you feel a bit "on the spot." You are the department head and you haven't prepared as well as you would have liked, or feel you have to prove yourself in some way. You feel under pressure, a bit scared and very tense.

Now imagine that you could stop and think, "I need to be fully present and neutral here." You could bring your attention to the feeling of your feet on the floor, then to your breath, then notice the tension in your shoulders and relax them. You briefly move your Awareness to Being Aware and realize that you are connected to every aspect of what you are about to encounter and that if you maintain a positive, neutral attitude, you intend that everything works out positively for your benefit. You take a final big breath, exhale and open the door. Can you feel how just those few moments of being aware could make a huge difference in the outcome of the meeting?

CHAPTER 5

Exploring the Structure of the Ego:
Your False Self

In order to look at how to clear up the past, we need to know the structure of the Ego and the Context it lives within.

From a spiritual perspective, we <u>have</u> a body and a personality, yet for most of us, most of the time, we <u>are</u> our body and personality, so we had better understand the nature of what we inhabit. It is like having the owner's manual for the car you drive.

Imagine, once again, that you have been holding onto the rearview mirror, driving through life. You would be wondering why you have so many accidents (dramas, fights, arguments, and other unhappy experiences). Most of us operate in life based on the rearview mirror of our past experiences – patterns of behavior that just seem to take us over. It would be a good idea to get your hands on the steering wheel, as that is how the car works. It is the same with us in our lives. We need the operating manual to learn how and what works.

Three Aspects to the Ego

There are three aspects of "who you consider yourself to be." Your **BODY**, your **MIND,** with your individual life experiences, and your **BELIEFS** about yourself and the world you live in: all three work together to form the majority of your identity and behavior patterns.

A good analogy would be a computer with its hard drive wiring, its operating system and its unique software and data. Only the software and data give a sense of uniqueness. Everything else functions exactly the same for all computers.

Your **BODY** is the current result of millions of years of evolution and is hard wired for one thing only, **SURVIVAL**. If you study the nervous system, it becomes apparent that all sensory perceptions, sight, touch, sound, taste and smell, first arrive at the most primitive part of the brain, the Amygdala. In the Amygdala, a pre-cognitive process of screening takes place. It asks, "Is this a threat to survival or not?"

You can see this play out in watching a lizard (scientists often call the Amygdala, the lizard brain). If a shadow passes over a lizard that is eating or looking for food, the lizard will immediately do one of three things. Prepare to fight, flee (scamper away), or freeze. After all, the shadow may be a hawk looking for lunch.

If it was a cloud, it was a false alarm and is no big deal. The lizard can afford many "false positive," indications and do their survival reactions but no false negatives. Therefore, it will tend to react to anything close to the possibility of a hawk shadow. This feature of reaction to a possible threat is hard wired into the lizard's system and is likewise hard wired into our physical, biological system, which we inhabit.

There is a story about Charles Darwin, after having determined that biologically nature was wired for survival, thought that perhaps he could train his system not to react to a certain stimulus. So, he repeatedly visited the cobra cage in the zoo and, putting his face up against the glass, tried not to jump backwards when the cobra struck the glass. He could never stop the automatic reaction, even though he knew what was coming.

I am not sure all of our reactions are quite so automatic, once we are able to recognize them. However, it is important to understand how out of our control these initial reactions are. They occur prior to the stimulus reaching the part of the brain where we become aware and are able to think. This will be an important distinction when we finally look at how to clear up our past conditioning, especially our dysfunctional patterns of behavior.

The internal reaction to a perceived threat is what most of us generally call fear. It has predictable survival- oriented responses, including; tightness in the stomach, wanting to defecate, increased heart rate, with perhaps tightness across the chest and sweaty palms, pumping more blood to major muscles (experienced as heat) for fight or flight, cold clammy palms as the blood rushes to the large muscles and a heightened sense of alertness. All of these physical reactions would be very helpful, if confronted with a saber-toothed tiger, when real danger was present.

Why is it then, that most of us feel those same reactions when asked to give a public presentation, when there is no physical danger and audiences stopped throwing rotten tomatoes several centuries ago? This brings us to the next elements of our ego, our mind and our social identity.

The **MIND** is also dedicated to survival and integrally connected to the body. If you examine your own mind, (difficult I know), I think you will find that the mind consists of a stack of three dimensional, multi-sensory images, that seem to be arranged in chronological order. These images give us the sense of time and the sense of our own continuity in the story, we call our history.

Obviously, we remember some and not every memory from this stack of images, with their records of body sensations, emotions, thoughts, what happened, smells, sounds, etc., a total record. This has been proven in some post-operative therapy sessions, where even though the patient was unconscious, the patient recorded everything that was happening.

It is also obvious that we may agree with others as to what generally happened and when, yet we can be quite different in our interpretations of what happened. As you become more conscious, you may see that this bias or interpretation is a function of your beliefs. Also, the stack of images is where your knowledge is stored and where you look for what is appropriate in any given situation – a useful function of the memory bank.

Whether useful or counter-productive, the mind's primary function is to help you survive, first as your body and next because they are intertwined, your social persona. Therefore, it records your reactions to any traumas, injuries or threatening situations, in which you did survive, as necessary for your future survival. You are reading this so you obviously survived your life experiences up until now. Here is how it works.

Anytime the current environment is at all similar (cloud looks like a hawk's shadow) to the situation of the earlier trauma, injury or threat, whatever was done, felt, sensed, determined in thought, then needs to be repeated once again, in a totally mechanical fashion. Repeating the pattern supposedly assures survival. This is important. The repeated pattern will include all the physical sensations, all the emotions like fear, rage, shame, etc. and the original thoughts that were present, like; "I deserve this," or "I can't trust her," or "the world isn't safe," or "I am no good."

Sometimes these decisions we made are upgraded to a more sophisticated, current version, with lots of explanation and reasons attached. For example, "I deserve this," might have lots of reasons for failing, blame of others, and excuses for your own behavior. The feelings and body sensations, however, will be the same as in the earlier trauma.

You could be throwing an adult version of a tantrum you threw at three years old when you had colic and your mother was not there to take care of you. You feel the same old feelings that you have been abandoned, or ignored, or rejected. Your needs are not being met. You are not valued or respected.

Now, perhaps the rage is suppressed, yet still present and comes out as some form of passive aggressive behavior. It is still a repeated pattern, assuring survival and almost assuredly not producing aliveness, love or happiness.

The body sensations are repeated as tension and stomach upset, perhaps after being repeated so often that by now you have an ulcer. The thoughts are judgmental and blaming of whomever is the current person (similar to) your mother who you were originally mad at for leaving you, not feeding you, etc.

Just as originally you blamed what your mother did for how you feel, you now blame the person who triggered your reaction as being the cause of your reaction. Just another false cause explanation for your internal experience.

The replay of this pattern is called an **UPSET**. And the upset reinforces, strengthens and gets added to the original behavior pattern in kind of a linked chain of times when you repeated this pattern. Also, the similarity potential expands as first mother, then wife, or other women all get lumped together as potential threats to be on the lookout for.

This is how people who might be afraid of one person early in life, through some trauma, like physical or sexual abuse, become more and more paranoid as they get older, until they are generally afraid and limit their life out of this expanded fear.

It can get to the point where you are literally sleep walking through life, unconscious, totally identified with who you consider yourself to be, reacting to various stimuli in a perpetual set of upsets and repeated patterns. These patterns all have a degree of suffering and unhappiness imbedded in them. You are quite literally a stimulus–reaction machine, like a jukebox, playing the same song when the B3 button gets pushed.

The Journey of Liberation

The first step on the journey of liberation is to acknowledge the extent to which you are reacting rather than responding, righteous and defensive rather than understanding, avoiding confrontations and hiding rather than stepping out and confronting issues.

Look at how you might want to be loving with family members and after a few days together, you are reactivated in dysfunctional, unhappy patterns of feelings, thoughts and behaviors from the past.

Perhaps it is repeated patterns that you notice in relationships, or in your career, school, about your body, eating, weight, etc.

Exercise

Take out your journal and for each domain deepen your insight and understanding of how you "show up," when things clearly aren't working. It is essential as we go onto what is next, to take the time to write these descriptions in your journal.

1. When do you get angry, annoyed, or frustrated?
2. When do you get depressed, sad, or feel hopeless?
3. When do you experience yourself being right and making others wrong?
4. Do you avoid being controlled or told what to do?
5. Are you controlling, domineering, or arrogant?
6. Do you sometimes feel alone and not appreciated or respected?
7. What do you do to avoid situations?

Your job is to identify these patterns in your own life, as acknowledging that you have them will be necessary in understanding and applying this material in your life, where it counts.

This is how you start to Wake Up and Face Up to this entity you call "ME." So, tell the unvarnished truth to yourself. You don't have to share it with anyone and you don't have to prove that everything is OK or try to fit in and be accepted. And this is not the total picture of who you are, but it is the times when things are not working and you are unhappy. This is the entry way to the shadow work. So, describe what happens and feel the feelings.

The Nature of Beliefs

This next section ties together the Conversation (the ongoing play) you were born into, the Agreement Reality we discussed above and your beliefs. It is important to emphasize that most of your current beliefs were acquired entirely unconsciously and already existed in the Illusionary Bubble Reality you were born into.

You just took them on because it was necessary to fit in and be accepted in your family, school, religion, neighborhood and society. This is how the sins of the parents are passed down from generation to generation. Where else did the cultural norms, both good and bad come from? Or the prejudices held by children with no previous experiences that would justify those prejudices? Sometimes, it is easy to see these prejudices and biases in others, like antisemitism, racial or gender bigotry and it's not always so easy to see them in ourselves.

There are two aspects about beliefs. A belief is either a concept about what you are not experiencing directly or an interpretation of current reality.

For example, when you walk from one room to the next, the reality of the old room turns into the form of a belief, a mental picture, a concept, not a direct experience. On the other hand, examples of your interpretation would be some distrust of all men, or a distrust of women's emotions, or a fear of some race or tribe and the tribal or racial superiority of your own. Or having a belief that there aren't enough resources for everyone (a scarcity mentality).

Once you have a certain belief, you will collect evidence that supports that belief, and in some instances, only see evidence supporting that belief. This is an important distinction: <u>you only see the evidence that tends to support a belief you already have</u>. The belief then gets pasted onto the physical reality and collapses into the physical reality so that it is no longer seen as your interpretation of reality, it becomes, for you, reality itself.

Perception Reinforces Beliefs

It is a challenging fact to our strongly held beliefs, especially when we think the facts we are using to justify our belief confirm its veracity, that we may only be seeing what confirms our belief, not the whole picture.

Start with this example:

"Aoccdrnig to rscheearch at Cmabrigde Uinervtisy, it deosn't mttaer waht oredr the ltteers in a wrod are,

the olny iprmoetnt thing is taht the frist and lsat ltteer be in the rghit pclae. The rset can be a ttoal mses and you can sitll raed it wouthit a porbelm. Tihs is bcuseae the mnid deos nto raed ervey lteter by istlef, but the wrod as a whole."

I know you saw the jumble of letters yet notice how easily you understood the message. There is some recent research that says we only need about ten percent raw data and the mind connects the dots, so to speak, just like a computer decompression program, to create our total multi-sensory reality.

The vase/two face example below demonstrates that while you will be able to see each in turn, a vase or two faces, you will not be able to see them both at once. As only one version of reality can exist is any moment of now. Try it out.

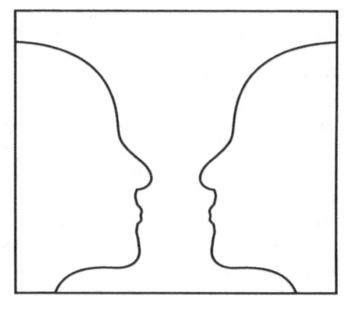

In viewing optical illusions like the vase/two faces, it is not so much that we have the power to switch our perception from one "what I see" to another but that your mind is doing that kind of selective seeing all the time. Further, if we are attached to a certain way we know the world is, the reptilian brain will make sure that we only receive evidence supporting that particular view.

Taken to the extreme, an Albert Einstein quote speaks to this: "*A human being is a part of the whole called by us universe, a part limited in time and space. He experiences himself, his thoughts and feeling as something separated from the rest, a kind of optical delusion of his consciousness.*"

Yet don't we only see evidence for this separateness? Or at least live out of that reality even when there may be some evidence to the contrary?

All your beliefs shape your behavior and are mostly an attempt to gain certainty and permanence and a feeling of security in an otherwise changing and uncertain world. Most beliefs are fear based and, as I mentioned before, the more rigidly held and the more righteous in their defense, the more fearful the belief holder. Beliefs and the strategies and actions they justify can be driven by fear of chaos, of being out of control, of being wrong, of being dominated by others, of being abandoned or rejected, even terror of being totally helpless or powerless. The actions you take supposedly counter these fears and are justified by the beliefs. The belief is stable, certain, something "solid," to hold onto when, in fact, it is only a thought form trying to protect you from a changing Agreement Based Reality.

You have probably heard the adage that *the only constant is change itself,* yet we rigidly stick to and defend beliefs even when the defense or righteous propagation of the belief seems to create animosity, distance between people, even hate.

Look at religions, which are themselves based on some interpretation, some belief. How many wars, how much killing, how much hatred, how much sense of superiority and subjugation of others has been justified by religious beliefs which are supposedly about love and God? This is just an obvious example.

The mechanism of being right about our/my beliefs is the same for all of us, just more subtle perhaps in people who are not so obviously justifying their behavior. When you judge another, when you criticize, when you see yourself as better than others, these too are based on beliefs. So, keep the self-inquiry going.

Exercise

What are your most rigidly held beliefs? Look to times when you felt more distant from another, more dislike, or didn't want to be with them anymore. What beliefs were present in those incidents? Beliefs can be some of your most dearly held notions of who you are, versus who they are. They can be some version of, "I am a good person and they are evil." A good question to ask, when looking into your assumptions and beliefs is, "Is it true?"

Continue your lists of beliefs for each domain in your journal. See if you would say, "but that is just the way it is."

Are you a Belief?

How does this all relate to you, your ego and the world you live in? First off, who you consider yourself to be, the social persona, the ego, has all the elements of a belief. It is a concept composed of many identities cobbled together, mother, wife, child, parent, teacher, lawyer, athlete, successful, loser, etc. Then you have your age now versus who you were at say two or eight or as a teen. Almost nothing is the same. It all changed. Yet, we say that story, that history is "ME."

All these concepts/beliefs get stripped away when you start asking Ramana Maharshi's question, "Who am I?" With the response, "Not that." Also, there are the beliefs you hold about other people and the world at large that fit together and are compatible with your concept of yourself.

For example, to justify being shy, you might hold the belief that others are domineering bullies and don't care about you or your ideas. Or if you are a controlling, aggressive, know-it-all type, your notion of others would have to be that they are not very smart, need your strong hand and you are contributing to them with the gift of your knowledge. You don't listen to their point of view, or you discount it, and seem to constantly have to deal with people who are incompetent and don't really like you. You get the picture.

My point is that we live in a total world of language, concepts and beliefs and we hold onto them as kind of a security blanket. Otherwise to the separate ego self, the chaotic, changing, uncertain world would bring up enormous fear and anxiety. As long as you identify with this thing you call, "Me," you will be subjected to the many aspects of this survival based Illusionary reality.

Beliefs are a survival mechanism. I am not saying we have to get rid of all beliefs, however, some are very limiting for creating what we want. Those would be good to replace with more positive beliefs that will allow for a more positive experience of life.

Two Core Mistakes of, "I as a Thing"

Returning to our conversation about the Illusion and the several fundamental mistakes or misperceptions that we tend to operate from, like "false cause" which we have discussed, the <u>most fundamental mistake</u> is the belief that, "I am this body with this personality and this history. That who I am is a Thing."

Yes, your body is your current piece on the chess board of life. And you will be using it as your vehicle for the rest of your life. So, it is important to really understand your body's nature at its core, its limitations and its abilities.

This insight I will share with you took me many years to see, as it is kind of like looking back at yourself from your current self. Had I really accepted this years ago, I am certain my life would have turned out differently. By sharing it with you, hopefully you can speed up your process.

Most of us have a degree of insecurity that we are trying to hide on one hand, and to overcome on another. For many years on my path, I missed the incredible power of the two declarations I will discuss below, that form the core of the ego structure and create so much unhappiness, struggle, dysfunction and suffering in our lives.

The first is, **"I am separate."** This declaration was something that obviously already existed in the culture. You did not make it up! However, you did agree with it and in so doing, it became the first building block of your identity. The "I am," part is the key. It defines who you are, as only you, in the end, have the power to determine. It is the method, through declaration, of creating something out of nothing, out of the empty awareness that you truly are.

You of course were trained, cajoled and coerced into it – given a name, and taught the separate names of every other thing. You became separate in a world of separateness. Now along with this declared separateness comes the contrasting fear of annihilation and the intense desire for connection.

At the beginning of your life, you felt very connected in the womb. With birth and the gradual solidification of the notion of being separate comes the fear of rejection and abandonment, and to a certain extent, death and non- existence. Countering these fears, are the various strategies to gain connection, acceptance and some form of love. Whether by trying to be admired through accomplishment or by giving up what you might want to do to be accepted and fit in. This is quite insane, as without this mistaken core foundation to your identity, you would have some sense that you are already connected to everything.

In 2009, I had the good fortune to visit the Achuar

community in the Amazon jungle between Peru and Ecuador, as a guest of two of the founders of the Pachamama Alliance, Bill and Lynne Twist. This trip gave me the unique opportunity to experience a people who lived in a reality that was not based on the extreme sense of separation that we live in, rather a more connected, cooperative reality.

While the Pachamama Alliance has been helping the Achuar defend their territory against oil and timber exploitation, the Achuar community told us, we could use their help, as we are living the wrong dream - a dream based on separation rather than connection.

They claim that all of our ills are a function of living out of that dream based on separation - social injustice, treating each other badly; environmental degradation, treating our planet as if it was some separate, dead, throw away resource. And that we live in a spiritual vacuum which we try to fill with the accumulation of more and more stuff. Even the "God," we pray to is separate!

I am not claiming that the Achuar are perfect, as even they used to engage in raids and mini wars over a stolen woman or a territorial dispute, however, it is interesting that they live in a more connected reality, to each other and to their environment, and like the sages in India identify it as, "living in a dream."

This separateness is a powerful force that drives behaviors like giving up your voice, your self-expression, or what you want to do, to fit in and be accepted. People have gone to their graves lamenting that they never fully expressed their true selves.

Exercise

Once again take out your journal and consolidate what you are noticing about yourself which could be driven by this core declaration of who you are.

What have you done or what do you do to fit in, to be accepted, to not be abandoned or rejected, to get some sense of love and connection? Sometimes this even takes the form of getting attention resulting from negative behaviors, (attention being a poor substitute for acceptance and love). As I said, this is a powerful dynamic, so spend a few moments seeing how much this has shown up in your life. Write your personal examples in your journal.

The ego survives by mechanically repeating patterns, the core of which is separation. By acting out of "I am separate," you will keep returning to the experience of being separate and alone. This becomes a place to escape to when relationships become challenging. Or a lonely, perhaps comfortable retreat, missing connection, but feeling secure in the familiarity of the aloneness.

How about when you were feeling very connected, loving, friendly and warm toward someone, then they said something or did something that upset you? You then judge them, and they become the enemy, one of the "them," and you experience being alone again. And you did it entirely in your internal experience, even though you blamed the breach of connection on what they said or did. People commit suicide from this alone hopeless place, when the next mistake I present compounds the experience and it all becomes too overwhelming.

The second mistake is some form of, **"I am not OK."** Again, this belief that the world is flawed, needs fixing because it is not perfect, and not OK was in the conversation you were born into. If the world is flawed, then of course you are too.

And it is easy to conclude this when you are the little kid who doesn't know the answers and is less competent than the older kids or the adults. So, you did not make this one up either. But again, by your agreeing to it, you declared it into existence with the "I am," part. This Not OKness can take many forms and it is useful to find your version.

Some of the versions of Being Not OK are:
- not worthy
- not acceptable
- unlovable
- invisible
- not capable
- insufficient
- not good enough
- flawed
- broken
- not perfect
- a screw up
- stupid
- unwanted
- don't belong
- must be something wrong with me.

Exercise

See if you can determine what your version might be and write it in your journal. It may be a combination of several. For me it was "not good enough" and "there must be something wrong or missing in me." It will certainly be something you wouldn't want to admit: something you have been hiding, denying or trying to overcome.

In the second grade, I was the kid who couldn't read, who got beaten up by the big boys and who was the last kid chosen for games on the playground, with a comment like, "Who wants Carter?"

I had headaches at school and wore glasses to help me read. Note: at age 79, I do not need glasses, so what was that about? I ran away from school several times, even threw a shoe at the teacher in my frustration. It was not a very promising start!

Luckily, I had a supportive mother who took me aside and somehow instilled in me that I was able. Perhaps, it was her slightly superior attitude that said I was also somehow superior, because in my attempt to meet her expectations, I went on to become the youngest Eagle Scout in Minnesota and to excel in sports and school.

I went to one of the most difficult boarding schools, Phillips Academy Andover, then onto Yale where I excelled, played three varsity sports and captained the ski team. Then I attended Harvard Business School, where I captained the Rugby team. All in all, a successful growing up.

However, as I look at it now, I was always nervous and under pressure to succeed. I remember before the kickoff for the Yale/Princeton game, I was on the field and took my mouthpiece out and threw up, in front of 70,000 people!

I can see that the effort to overcome who I considered myself to Be, at my core, "Not Good Enough," drove me to successes. But it also led to wanting to be in control and to being way too competitive later in life, in situations in which cooperation would have been more productive. So yes, I got something out of that inadequacy, yet it didn't lead to a sense of fulfillment or completeness or sustained happiness.

I always felt there was something wrong with me, but never could figure out what it was. Now I see the dynamics clearly.

What is your version of "Not OK?" How has it motivated your accomplishments? Or on the other side, how has it periodically been confirmed through negative results in your life? Like a failure in business or relationships, where you end up depressed and sad and once again feeling, "I am not good enough."

Remember, the EGO has only one purpose and that is survival, which means the continuation of what you have decided you are and what the world is. Along with the declaration of, "I am Not OK," and its diminished sense of Self are several emotions:

- shame
- sadness
- guilt
- feeling invalidated
- less than
- feeling invisible
- frustration

- fear of being out of control
- fear of rejection and abandonment
- fear of failure
- feeling you deserve punishment.

As you look to see what your version of "Not OK," is, expect to also get in touch with some emotions you have been resisting most of your life. Remember, we operate out of our emotions – trying to feel better when we are feeling bad. Resisting feeling these "negative," emotions is a natural consequence of your inbred, unexamined strategy to somehow overcome those emotions.

Yet, <u>what you resist persists</u> and these emotions therefore run you by motivating dysfunctional patterns such as:

- being righteously right
- justifying your actions
- controlling and dominating others or the situation
- avoiding being dominated or controlled
- hiding your self-expression (your light) under the proverbial bushel basket from fear of being criticized, embarrassed, rejected, or abandoned.

From the perspective of clearing up your past, <u>it is essential that you get in touch with those uncomfortable feelings</u>. For what you can experience and "let be," will let you be free. It is a counter-intuitive, yet a positive move on the Path toward Freedom.

I remember that at 13 months when my brother was born, my mother's attention and nurturing turned away from me. I felt betrayed and abandoned and in turn pulled away from her, so not to be hurt like that again. Of course, by then I had already decided I must be "not good enough," otherwise why would she abandon me, which got reinforced at school and on the playground.

I still wanted my mother's love and approval, which came out of the desire for connection, even though I had decided, "I am separate." I struggled to always be the favored child (out of three brothers) by being the best. To get her approval, acceptance and praise was my modus operandi. This pattern was very dysfunctional in my first marriage, when "look how great I am," was neither appreciated nor nurturing and loving for my wife.

I always carried around a fear of failure or being rejected. I remember in my twenties, walking into a restaurant and sweating under my arms as I wondered what people were thinking of me. Pretty insecure I know, but I put on a pretty good facade to cover the insecurity.

Also, I was very competitive and dismissive with my younger brother and in some regards competitive with my father to get my mother's love/approval/acceptance, which set up a pattern of unhealthy competition with other males in work situations.

Now would be a good time to take out your journal again and list more examples from your life. Perhaps rereading the above so that the lists of possible experiences and questions will trigger some memories you hadn't yet noticed. So, take your time working on this section. And feel some compassion for yourself in those difficult situations. Know, you were doing the best you could do at those times.

Your Success Strategies

Once those two basic declarations (I am separate and not OK) are in place, which fundamentally define your Ego based personality, you will see that they have been the drivers for what we call "your success strategy,," or "your winning formula," although often it is not too winning!

You need something, some persona, some way of being that covers over the secret truth you feel about yourself. Imagine approaching someone to introduce yourself. "Hi, I'm lonely, afraid you will reject me, not good enough, inadequate Landon. I deserve to be rejected and not accepted, because why would you want to be with such a failure of a human being, someone flawed like me?"

It just isn't going to get us the connection and

acceptance we so desperately desire, so we all put on a somewhat false facade (a persona or mask), an image we present to the world, that covers up the basic hidden truth of who we are afraid we are and at the same time, who we consider ourselves to be.

The agreement becomes: "If you buy my B.S., I will buy yours." It goes something like, "Hi I'm Landon, graduate of three of the best schools in the US, captain of sports, Peace Corp volunteer, successful in this or that job, blah, blah, blah." You get the picture. Now I can't brag about it, as I wouldn't want to look too arrogant however, I will drop enough hints and names for you to get the picture. And of course, you would want to know me as I extend my hand in greeting!

Putting It All Together

So, let's pull the pieces together now and add a few more corollaries. As we covered, your Body is your piece in the game of life. It is wired for survival, which shows up at the most primitive level as Five F's: fight, flight, freeze, feed, and fornicate. This is the first part of your identity.

Next is the conceptual, social self which we are calling your Ego. This extends beyond the body and yet is bonded to the body for its physical and emotional expression. This social persona lives in a world of language, conversations, interpretations and beliefs, who you say you are, who other people are and your notion of the world at large. It includes things like:

- my reputation
- my principles
- my history
- my story
- my fatherhood
- my husband hood
- my beliefs of what is right and wrong, good and bad
- my sports team
- my army platoon
- my country, etc.

It is anything with a "Me," or "My," attached to it.

As we have already discussed, the entire structure of the Ego is dedicated to only one thing, survival. Even though you say you want love, happiness, and peace, those are the first things that seem to be given up as your survival-oriented ego expresses itself in the social arena. <u>Fight</u> shows up as being right and making others wrong, of defending your point of view, of invalidating others, of controlling and dominating the situation and avoiding being dominated. Also, judging others as inferior and being better than them through some sort of prejudice or bias.

One of the first things to confront on the path is how committed you are to being Right, sometimes to the extent of being "Dead Right" meaning no aliveness at all in your interactions. If you want aliveness and happiness, you will have to give up your righteousness, as happiness and having to be right are incompatible.

Flight shows up as avoidance, withdrawal, acting out of the fear of disapproval. Freeze may show up as doing whatever it takes to not be rejected, submitting to situations you don't agree with and you are too afraid to speak up about.

And if the negative feelings get too bad, you can always Feed, drink alcohol or get addicted to drugs to suppress the feelings. Or get high for a short time, to avoid the negative feelings. Or get addicted to sex Fornicate for a few moments of relief.

As strange as it seems, these are all patterns of behavior that ensure survival of your ego, because the ego survived in the past and survives by repeating patterns. Repetition is what gives some continuity to this Thing called "Me."

It would be useful to notice how committed you are to being right, to justifying your actions (again to be right), to avoiding situations, or tending to withdraw into your separate self. If you pay attention, you can begin to catch yourself in these behaviors.

These actions are usually accompanied by physical sensations like tension, and emotions like anger and frustration which will probably bring out some fight reaction, arguing for your point of view. Or you may feel disappointment, disapproval, or rejection and withdraw from a situation and will righteously justify your actions. All of these strategies apparently lessen your bad feelings and ensure the survival of this ego structure, but the cost is your aliveness, full self-expression and happiness.

Keep acknowledging these behaviors and feelings, as they are the easiest experiences to become aware of and ultimately the most life changing entry points in this self- inquiry process.

I encourage you to give yourself time for self-discovery. Write down what you are discovering in your journal. And remember, keep going back through each domain to register, "how am I showing up here?" It will pay big rewards as we move along.

I know that I am asking you to admit to yourself all the negative, dysfunctional behaviors you probably have been working on and want to overcome and maybe feel some shame about. I know it is counter intuitive, remember the mantra, "the way out (to freedom) is through," to choose to consciously experience your experience. You have to begin to own (take responsibility for) how you have been showing up in the world to be able to let those patterns go.

Once you begin to tell the truth to yourself about how you act in different domains of your life, like how you relate to your body, or what happens in relationships at home and at work, then you are ready to discover what is driving these behaviors.

You will also become fully aware of who you consider yourself to be. You must admit to yourself this shadow side of your personality. For in doing so, "the truth shall set you free," of the very barriers to the happiness you desire and deserve.

I know I keep emphasizing your negative aspects. And I know there are many wonderful positive qualities about you as well - loving, generous, contributing, enthusiasm, etc. However, your greatest learnings will come from, and the greatest difference will be made to your life by examining these negative, dysfunctional patterns. So, trust me a bit here and keep doing the shadow work.

The Wiley Ego

The material you are learning is within the teachings of Jnana Yoga, using the mind to understand and uncover the truth behind the mind. The Yogic tradition considers it to be the fast path to enlightenment and it is also a potentially dangerous path. Once you know the truth of the way your mind works and the way the Illusion operates, your ego can take over. It then uses the information to enhance itself and be right, as it makes others into the problem and denies its own responsibility. Looking back, I can see how I dealt with my wife in the 1980's. I was the know-it-all trainer from est, who had trained 50,000 people. I didn't know then what I know now and what I am passing onto you through this handbook.

However, I knew enough and was denying and hiding (unconsciously) my own insecurities, my not good enough. In some regards, my wife and I were operating at the wrong level, trying to solve relationship problems without going to the heart of who we were and our insecurities.

We just didn't know enough to actually get to what was causing our problems. Often, I remember feeling quite hopeless when she would withdraw from me. I am sure I made her wrong for what was the current issue. She was the problem, she needed to change.

In my arrogance, I had lots of information and reasons to justify the rightness of my position. That is the dangerous part of this path. The ego will grab onto any identity (the trainer for me) or information to survive. An easy indication is whenever you are feeling "better than," and making someone else "less than," the ego is at play.

It is therefore essential that you use this information to gradually see and to let go of the hold your own ego has on you. You can do that by admitting what is true for you, by exploring in your self-inquiry the very nature of your ego structure and how your mind sabotages your reality.

This is where real responsibility starts and where the light shines at the end of the tunnel of unconsciousness and darkness.

The EGO's two core mistaken beliefs (declarations) "I am separate," and "I am Not OK," drag along a whole plethora of unpleasant, negative emotions that become part of your identification of who you consider yourself to be at your core - this flawed, broken, imperfect person. Sometimes we see our version of "Not OK," yet resist feeling the emotions fully that accompany it and therefore can't quite heal this fundamental aspect of our ego nature. So, as you go through this list, let yourself consciously feel the emotions that fit for you. Volitionally, explore what you have been resisting feeling and be the curious Observer. In the same way you consciously observed your thoughts in the meditation practice, this time let the emotions resonate in your body.

As you feel the feelings, you might recall early traumatic experiences which either initiated the feelings or reinforced them. This is part of the process. You just got stuck with your version of "I am Not OK" and the accompanying feelings, which became part of your identity. So, take your time as you go through this list.

- fear
- hurt
- invalidation
- worthlessness
- shame
- sadness
- grief
- rage
- discouragement
- hate
- despair
- powerlessness
- hopelessness

As we have discussed, the desire to avoid those unpleasant emotions generates the invention or adoption of a personality that denies these insecurities or core identification building blocks of your ego and avoids feeling these negative emotions.

Here is an example. You receive some criticism and start to feel hurt or invalidated. You avoid feeling those feelings when your ego jumps to your defense by getting angry and defensive, invalidating the criticizer. Or you go into a funk of depression which is a suppression of the anger you don't feel you can outwardly express. You fill in the blanks as to what you do when you get criticized. Time for your journal again.

This non-useful reaction to criticism is far from the possibility of being a learner, asking for feedback, and being energized and happy in the learning process. Quite the opposite, it is a fear-based survival pattern of the false identity, the Ego.

When you begin to see how you operate, you will also start to notice how others operate. And you will start to recognize that for the most part, you live in a survival- oriented world where the possibility of having what you want, happiness, just isn't a lasting possibility.

We live in a context of survival. That doesn't mean survival is the only possibility, it means that if you don't wake up and do something about it, you are destined, or should I say doomed, to live out of an unexamined **Survival Context** like water to the fish.

I won't go into all the examples you can find for living in a survival context. I leave that up to you. Besides looking at the amount of righteousness, justification, defensiveness, complaining and blaming you see, think about power, greed, the accumulation of stuff and wars. All are expressions of personal egos or a nation's ego expressing survival.

There is an alternative, once you get out of your own way, and that is to live a fully expressed, joyous, happy, loving life. The next step is how to clear up these patterns, this past conditioning, that keeps surfacing and repeating itself in our Present Life, Now.

Summary

You should have a fairly complete understanding of the structure of your EGO and how creating reality through that structure produces so much of the suffering and unhappiness in your life. You have always been a fully creative, powerful Being, it is just that you have been creating reality unconsciously through a structure dedicated to survival rather than happiness. Now we will use that understanding to transform your life. To clear up the past patterns of conditioned behavior and to create space for new ways of Being and new realities.

CHAPTER 6

Clearing Up The Past

Ultimately, clearing up the past involves seeing your ego patterns for what they are and withdrawing your identity from them. So that they become, at worst, something you have and are not who you are. It involves transcendence, in that you metaphorically rise above your old personality, you are not it, no longer that "Thing" you thought you were. And this allows for transformation to take place, as you have the ability to start to show up in a different form, a new way of Being.

All the elements we have discussed so far come into play, and yet it is a simple step of letting go of your attachment and letting things be as they are. Let's begin.

I need to reiterate that while simple, this process takes an enormous commitment:

- to telling the truth
- to your own evolution as a conscious, aware human being
- to being happy rather than being right
- to giving up your commitment to being comfortable
- to giving up your investment in looking good and having your act together

These are the life-long ego-based commitments that you need to let go of and tell the unvarnished truth about to yourself.

Keep putting your examples, your learnings and realizations in your journal. An important notion at this point of your inquiry is to assume that your current reality is a reflection of what you have been unconsciously creating and committed to. Ouch, not a fun thought!

You have never stopped being a creative Being. You have just been operating unconsciously through a dysfunctional ego structure. I know that is not a pleasant prospect when thinking about some of the domains in your life but it is the absolute first step in taking responsibility for your life.

Four Steps
There are four steps and some sub-steps that will guide you through the process of clearing up the past.

They are:
- Recognize
- Take Responsibility
- Discover
- Let go/Forgive

I will expand on each step of this process.

Recognize

Look at life this way. If you are not happy, loving, content and satisfied then you are UPSET. Some unconscious pattern is playing out in your life that is preventing you from having those positive experiences.

Happiness becomes the commitment and the mirror to see when you are not happy. Most people just breeze along, oblivious to the possibility they could even be happy, because it is so normal not to be.

They continue sleep walking through life, unconscious automatons reacting to the various stimuli that set them off. They blame the circumstances, criticize and blame others and life for their internal unhappiness.

YOU HAVE TO WAKE UP FROM THIS TRANCE.

And interestingly enough, noticing you are UPSET is the perfect "wake up call," and the doorway to freedom. This already entails a bit of detachment, as you start to become the witness to how your ego is showing up.

This is where your meditation practice starts to have a real benefit in your life. You need the strength to see what you thought was you for what it actually is, just a concept, with no solid self anywhere in the picture. Being able to let go of thoughts that seem to capture your attention is the practice which gets expanded to include, your emotions, your body sensations and finally your reactive behaviors that are driven by these experiences. So, keep at your meditation practice to build the strength to keep "Waking Up," and being able to transcend your dysfunctional patterns.

There is a shift in your language that is helpful in this process. Suppose you get angry. Instead of saying, "I am angry," shift to "I have anger."

Take Responsibility
There are two steps. This first step challenges most people, as they don't want the upset and therefore resist it happening. Most of us when upset immediately look for how we can fix the problem, or who to blame, or how to avoid it happening again.

This is what resistance looks like.

If you are committed to transforming your life, you need to shift this as you will never be able to clear it up by resisting it. So, the question really is: Are you willing to hold being upset as an <u>opportunity rather than a problem</u> to be solved, suppressed or gotten rid of?

The upset is the doorway to freedom. Only by it manifesting in your current experience are you able to get in touch with it, which is the start of being able to deal with it. So welcome upsets, as painful as they are, and recognize that there is divine perfection when they show up, given your desire and commitment to evolve into a more loving, happy person.

You are learning to re-contextualize the upset from "this is a problem" to "<u>this is an opportunity.</u>" This allows two important things to open up for you. One it allows you to <u>not resist the upset</u> and to start to be curious about how your own mind sabotages your experience.

And two, it makes the upset an integral part of your life's journey toward more consciousness, happiness, love and connection to everything.

This orientation is essential in intimate relationships if you want your relationship to continue to deepen and prosper.

Be a Happy Victim

The next step is to recognize that the starting place for any upset is feeling like a victim of some outside circumstance, or what someone says or does. Get comfortable with that victim starting point. You are shifting your perspective from "the upset has me," to "I have the upset."

Then again shift your perspective to "I am responsible for what I brought to the situation." This is where your insight into your version of "I am not OK," along with the accompanying emotions and behaviors come in. For example, I was this "angry, irritated, hurt, not good enough," waiting to get triggered, so I could react and reinforce my ego's survival. You will then also start to see what behaviors you did that allowed or furthered the situation.

Here are important questions to stop and consider:
- Are you really willing to take your full power back?
- Are you willing to be the total creator of your reality?
- Are you willing to at least look at your life from the perspective of being responsible?

If the answer is "YES," then you start that process by exploring how you are creating your current reality or drawing reality to you by Being the way you are.

The best place to start the process of clearing up the past is to look into the dysfunctional, unhappy, dissatisfying parts of your life. Use the negative to create the positive. To have what you desire, you will need to be fully your conscious creative self and this is the path. Through the darkness, your shadow side, you will come to the light. This brings us to the next step.

Discovery

The process of discovery involves the self-inquiry we have been leading you through in the previous chapters. You now have an opportunity, through recognizing and being willing to experience, but not necessarily acting out of, your upsets.

If you allow yourself to experience the upset and don't resist it, this can become the next step in your path to freedom. Embrace it. If you look back through your life, you will find that there have been numerous occasions where you felt this same upset. Not necessarily the same circumstances, but the same body sensations, the same emotions and feelings, the same thoughts and the same conclusions about yourself were present.

There is a method to help in this inquiry called the

Discovery Process. It is a combination of regression to earlier similar incidents and clearing each one by consciously causing yourself to experience the experiences that are associated with each incident.

The emotional charge and attachment to that incident as part of your identity lessens and can, in fact, totally be released when experienced fully with presence and awareness.

If you are very mindful and aware, the discovery step can and will occur in the process of your daily living. You will be going through the pattern in a conscious way, gradually detaching your True Self from it. Like the actor extracting herself from the role and returning to freedom of choice as to how she will show up.

Often, we are confronted with unwanted patterns of conditioned behavior, emotions and thoughts, which are so overwhelming that we need a more focused approach for discovering how the patterns are structured and held together. The following Discovery Process is designed to allow you to observe a pattern in a little more organized fashion.

This is a powerful process that you may find yourself doing often, so it is helpful to learn the steps.

Discovery Process
Read this exercise through to get an idea of the

sequence and then do it with your eyes closed. Alternatively, have a friend read the instructions as you do the process on some issue in your life. Your friend's job is to read the instructions aloud and not to give any advice or make any comments on what you say. An important part of doing this process successfully is to take whatever it is you get in response to the instructions. To observe whatever you see, sense or feel, without judging or assessing it as "right," or "wrong."

Start with an issue or problem in your life that you are experiencing or can vividly recall and would know when it went away. For example, let's suppose the problem is, "My relationship with my son. We always end up arguing and he never seems to listen to me or want my advice." Now as real as this might seem to you, the above, as stated, cannot be worked on very well as it is too conceptual and not experiential enough.

Using this example, you would ask yourself, "What exactly do I experience when my son and I get into an argument?" Using your power to observe, you will select some *item* (an aspect of your experience) that is very real for you. You might come up with an emotion, "my anger at my son," or "my sadness," or a body sensation that shows up as "a four-inch-wide band of tightness across my chest." The more specific you can be in defining your *item,* the better the process will work. Also, it must be something you experience directly, not what you do or what happens to others.

Next close your eyes and spend a few moments scanning your body internally with your consciousness to let go of any tension you have. Relax. Now repeat the *item* to yourself "my sadness...," or "the four-inch band...," or your friend can repeat the *item,* with each of the following instructions. You need to keep repeating the item to yourself throughout the process to stay focused on one item at a time and keep the mind bringing up only what is associated with that item. In terms of the model of the mind, your intention is to move back down the string of images that make up this pattern to its source, observing each experience as it surfaces.

Repeat the item. And ask yourself this question, "Am I willing to let go of the item?" If the answer is no, work on something else. You are not yet ready to give this up. Perhaps the payoff, what you get out of having it, is still too great. Something like your attachment to "father," who "knows best," and is "right." So, for now choose another item to work on that gives you a "yes," to the question.

When you decide on an item, rank its intensity on a scale from 1 to 10, which will give you a starting point and a way to measure your progress throughout the process.

Next repeat the item to yourself. Locate and describe a body sensation associated with the item. Locate another sensation and describe it, and another, and another until you have observed all that you are aware of. If you drift off, repeat the item to yourself and then take what you get in response to the question. Describe each sensation in terms of its location, size, shape, and the sensation itself e.g. "A two-inch diameter ball-shaped painful pressure one inch below the sternum."

Repeat the item to yourself and observe the emotions and feelings you have associated with the item. Ask, "What emotions and feelings do I have associated with the item?" Take whatever you see, sense or feel and allow yourself to experience it and go through the emotion while at the same time keeping your observer consciousness present. What other emotions do you experience associated with the item? Keep asking the question until you no longer experience a new emotion. You are in the process of taking an inventory of every aspect of experience associated with the item.

Next, repeat the item to yourself and observe the thoughts you have about it. What other thoughts do you have? What opinions? What judgments? What things have others said (friends, doctors, etc.)? What things have you read about the item? What decisions have you made about the item? Inventory your entire current mental realm, all thoughts, ideas, opinions, judgments, things others have said, attitudes, conclusions, and decisions.

Now repeat the item to yourself and locate an image from the past associated with the item. Take whatever you see, sense or feel in response to the instruction. If it is darkness, describe the darkness. If it is a general feeling of pressure, describe that feeling.

When you have an incident from the past (a memory) in mind, start at the beginning of the incident and go through it to the end, describing what happened. "He did this, I said that, she did......." As objectively as possible, describe what happened. Also, allow yourself to experience whatever emotions are there in the incident.

After you have gone through the incident once, go back to the beginning and go through it one more time, describing what happened, noticing if you missed anything. After observing that incident thoroughly from beginning to end, look to see if you made any decisions about yourself, other people, or the world at that time. If you experience an energy release, in that you have seen something you had not previously seen, and the pattern seems to have lifted, you might not need to go back any further. Check to see if the experience of the item has disappeared. If "Yes," open your eyes.

If not, repeat the item to yourself and "locate an earlier similar incident associated with the item." Again, take whatever you get and describe what you see, sense, or feel. Go through the incident describing what happened and then go back a second time describing what happened. Let yourself experience the emotions and feelings. Keep your Observer on, staying present, while you are reliving these past incidents. What decisions did you make about yourself, others, and the world in which you live? If you get a release, stop. If not, continue...

Repeat the item to yourself and locate a yet earlier similar incident associated with the item. Take what you get. How old are you? What happened? What decisions did you make if any? Keep going back until you get a release or run out of time.

A couple of comments: If you do not get a release during any single session, you will still get value out of the process, as any time you observe your experience you are in the process of clearing it up and releasing yourself and your energy from being trapped within the pattern. Observing the mind is like peeling an onion from the outside, only to reveal another layer underneath. Sometimes, having not reached the bottom of a pattern in a particular session, you may be more in touch with various aspects of the pattern than you were when you started—experiencing emotions of sadness or anger or feelings of depression, agitation, low self-esteem, and so on.

These feelings have always been a part of that pattern, stored in your mind/body and are now simply coming to the surface of your awareness. If you keep your observer on and continue to stay awake to your experience, these feelings will disappear in the process of you observing them over time. To do this, it is important to let them simply be the way they are without trying to change them in any way. If you try to change them, suppress them or resist them, they will persist.

Second, in doing the above process, you will never get more than you are able to handle. That doesn't mean that you won't experience intense emotions and relive old wounds. Only that what you experience has been inside you, suppressed and unconscious to be sure, but nonetheless totally active in replaying the automatic pattern and thereby running your life.

You have said that you are willing to let the pattern go and by implication, you are willing to look at its essential nature. You will therefore get the pattern in doses that you are capable of handling. If you somehow are not up to handling a portion of the pattern yet, the unconsciousness will put you to sleep or just shroud the key incident until the intensity of your observation can penetrate the unconsciousness. The only way out of these patterns is to go through them consciously. While it is not necessary to get every last detail, it is important to see how you are bringing past patterns to the current situation and that you are totally responsible as the owner of this aspect of who you consider yourself to be. It all started in some situation in your childhood, your past. Something happened, there were some highly charged emotions present (certainly for a baby or young child), and you decided something about yourself. You latched onto those emotions and that identity that seemed to justify the circumstance (like I am worthless, or invisible, or not good enough) and it became a part of who you considered yourself to be.

Only by seeing your conditioning and owning it, will you be able to let it go. You are in the process of going from being unconsciously stuck in the pattern, where it has you, to transcending the pattern to where you have it. After a number of times that the pattern gets reactivated, you will start to recognize it and have a shorthand label for it. Something like, "Oh, here is my not good enough showing up again."

This will allow you to either just let it go right then or to take some time to further explore, "what do I need to see about this pattern that I haven't yet experienced or seen?" In either case you will not be operating through the dynamics of the pattern and will have the choice to show up differently (Be different) and create a different reality.

Letting Go/Forgiving

This is the step in which you get to a Non-Reactive Neutral state. Here is where the practical application of your meditation practice of Being the Awareness, not the thought, or not the thinker, comes in handy.

Only with some degree of competence in this skill of being able to let go of thoughts, will you have the ability you need for this step. Letting go of a conditioned pattern that you have identified with most of your life is seemingly more complex with all its many dimensions than just letting go of a thought.

But the dynamics for letting go, the move you make, is the same. Ego patterns are made up of thoughts, memories, emotions, body sensations and behaviors, but in the end, it is all one thing – an ego pattern.

Letting go is also like **Letting It Be**. You are not trying to get rid of it per se or trying to override the pattern. Each of these moves only resists the pattern and **what you resist persists**, since in many regards, you are holding onto the pattern in order to push against it.

The counter-intuitive, yet successful move is to **Let It Be,** and just don't operate out of the pattern when you are Upset. It is kind of like having some handicap and you don't let it stop you.

Hale Dwoskin, founder of the Sedona Method, used to say, "letting go is as simple as holding up a pencil and just letting it drop." It still is in your space, yet you are no longer run by the pattern or your attachment to it.

A rule of thumb would be to *never try to solve the apparent problem or fix the situation until you are no longer upset.* Wait until you are in a Non-Reactive Neutral state. Only from this Neutral, in the Present Moment state do you start to see what is real and have a choice as to how you wish to respond and proceed.

Seeing the Perfection

As you gain insight into your own automaticity, you might also notice the perfection (I am not implying goodness) of the creative process, the karmic play we are all a part of. You will see that for the most part, people are just running their ego's patterns.

One person says "X," which pushes the "Y," button of the other person. We act like two juke boxes facing each other in which one provides the stimulus which elicits the reaction in the other, ad infinitum! Add two television sets on top of the juke boxes, both on automatic, talking away, no one listening, nobody home and you get a pretty good idea of what is really going on.

While at one level it is all perfect, unconscious gods creating all this drama, and eventually waking up, **Forgiveness** is a useful step in terms of making sure you really let go and are able to complete the past.

Around previous events, we often have resentments, regrets, guilt, shame, self-blame and blame of others. All of which occupy the emotional space within which you could be happy. These emotions, when they persist, can lead to "beating yourself up," in your self-talk, or harboring hate, resentment and anger for some past transgression by another.

Remember, you are committed to being happy and anything that gets in the way of that experience needs to be completed somehow and let go. For example, without condoning the abuse in any way, could you forgive an abuser by seeing that in some weird ego way he or she was trying to get some ego need met?

Like trying to get some form of connection, or just attention, or power over others. Or trying to fight his/her way out of a sense of being not good enough, out of control or helpless, or trying to overcome some form of inadequacy by diminishing another?

Knowing your own shadow side should help you have compassion, or at least more of an understanding, of why people do what they do. Take the words of Christ on the cross to heart, "Forgive them for they know not what they do." And you didn't either when you were unconscious! Try holding yourself as a LEARNER on the path to an enlightened, more evolved Self. How else would you know what to work on if you hadn't seen the pattern in action by living through it and creating the negative drama that you are now taking responsibility for and transforming?

To repeat the Carl Jung quote, *"One does not become enlightened by imagining figures of light, but by making the darkness conscious."* That is the Path.

An Ongoing Journey

Clearing up the past is an ongoing process. As you gain more consciousness by waking up to a pattern, owning it and letting it go, you will become aware of more subtle patterns in a seemingly never-ending process. You now have the tools and methodology to deal with unhappy patterns when they arise. This is something to be happy about.

As you move from a reactive state to a conscious presence, this gives you true Freedom of Choice to consciously create your experience at deeper and more subtle levels.

I am fortunate to have a partner in my wife Diane, who is willing to explore the workings of our minds together. We see how we trigger each of our increasingly deeper patterns. How the insecurity of my not being good enough and her not being seen or valued (invisible and worthless), play out in a perfect dance of revelation.

She is so courageous in bringing up things. She will say, "there's something I don't want to talk about." I so admire her courage. We wrote a book called, *Falling in Love Backwards: An Unlikely Tale of Happily Ever After*, that documents our process of resolving upsets and conflicts.

Our relationship did not get off to a great start by any normal standard, however by using these tools, it has only gotten better and better over the more than twelve years we have been together.

We sometimes have to pinch ourselves. How is it possible that we are more in love, more deeply connected, have more ecstatic love making, and feel more whole and complete within ourselves than when we started?

What I do know is that the experience we have is available to anyone who is willing to do the work. As all we are doing is returning to our true selves, which is the same Self for all of us.

And what we have is the natural outcome of being more and more in that Neutral Non-Reactive state from which we are creating more and more of the experience we want in life. I hope our example inspires you to continue the work, which I know can sometimes feel like the hardest work you will ever do, confronting your dark side and bringing it into the light.

I will say one more thing before moving on. Getting to a neutral state may feel a bit bland. Basically, throughout most of our lives we have been in reaction to circumstances and other people's comments and actions. And in many regards, we have become addicted to the emotional reactions those interactions and circumstances supposedly cause (false cause).

They have been the juice, the adrenalin, the spice – sadness, hate, anger, disappointment, hope, feeling high, excited, etc. so as you get to a Non-Reactive Neutral state, don't be too surprised if it may feel kind of blah.

It is from this nothingness, this aware emptiness that true creativity, passion, happiness, and joy come. Welcome this interim and necessary transitory state. It is a big step in your evolution.

CHAPTER 7

Living in the Present

We are always actually living in the present, however when the past impinges too heavily on the present moment, we need to use the tools we have learned to clear up the past. The same will be true when we look at worry and anxiety, as these are the result of projections into the future impinging on the present. We will get to that later. Now let's look at how to "Be Happy," in this moment.

The basic principle is **ACCEPTANCE.** This goes back to the teachings of the Buddha, in which he said that the world is filled with negative events like accidents, failures, sickness, and death, but you could eliminate the suffering you add to the events by accepting what is.

We don't normally accept things as they are. Rather we resist the experience and further hold it in place by adding an interpretation like, "this is bad, terrible, difficult, hurtful, shouldn't be happening, unfair." Or some meaning like, "this means I am no good, unworthy, deserve what happened to me."

Buddha characterized this Resistance as "grasping," for what you don't have (I want and I don't have a particular thing or experience) or "aversion," trying to push away what you do have or are experiencing.

Also, trying to hang onto something that is in its nature transitory, changing, and impermanent, like a pleasurable state. Every experience that is made up of physical, sensory, emotional, or thought forms is inherently temporary. It arises and it passes away.

To be happy you need to let life flow and not resist any aspect of it, including your interpretations. See them for what they are, just thoughts. Everything becomes what it is. This is it. You are Present and Accepting of it all. This is the <u>very essence of HAPPINESS</u>.

Being in the Flow

Having debunked the notion of false cause earlier in this handbook, I trust you realize that you are always trying to change internal experiences. A little pain or discomfort and you move to a more pleasant position. A negative, unpleasant emotion, and you try to change the circumstance or do something about it.

We even believe at some level that these negative

feelings and negative thoughts (I hate this, I am unhappy because of X, he or she shouldn't have done this or that, etc.) are the necessary motivators to changing things and in some regard, they are. However, if you examine the dynamics closely, you will see that you have allowed yourself to drift into some form of familiar dissatisfaction and unhappiness. Why is that?

Our Illusionary Reality has trained us to look for what is wrong and to try to fix it. We tend to reside in "this isn't it and I am dissatisfied," as our resident state. Sometimes this is quite strong, when we hate the situation and other times it can just be a low-level depressed resignation in the background of our life – that little dark cloud robbing you of being totally satisfied.

All this is suffering. Even if you do change the circumstance or situation, since you are **coming from** "this isn't it," the changes you do make are not very lasting or a permanent fix that can make you happy.

To accept things the way they are, both the situation you find yourself in and your internal experience, is not a passive act, like a victim surrendering to what seems out of his/her control. Rather, it is the first step, the very foundation, to the experience of happiness. Instead of resisting what is occurring, you are acknowledging that, "THIS IS

IT," and taking a responsible stand for that reality.

Again, look at it very closely. In this immediate moment of NOW, this nano second where all of living, being alive, takes place, can you actually change anything right NOW? If you are sitting down on your chair, can you not be sitting down?

Or take any aspect of this changing experiential reality. You have emotions and thoughts; can you really change them in this instant? That is not to say things don't change, they do, however, can YOU really change them NOW? Isn't it true that you only have a moment-by- moment glimpse of the way it is NOW? Be with that for a moment before going on.

This is so contrary to what we believe and what we have been taught and is why I originally said that each domain has its own dynamics. The reality of the PRESENT is that you can't change anything that is occurring, except perhaps how you are Being, how you hold the way it is, or how you are showing up as a conscious creator. I will say more on this later, in Creating Your Future.

So, what would make a difference in your life? Let me suggest that since what is occurring is unchangeable in this moment of your experience, that perhaps the only way to BE HAPPY is to surrender to the way it is.

Perhaps, try on the mantra,

"This too is what happiness looks like."

We are exploring being able to alter the context from which you look at the world and your internal experience. Kind of like being able to put on the proverbial "rose- colored glasses," that makes everything rosy.

I am not talking about being a Pollyanna here, just using your natural ability to shift your attention to a different perception of reality, which can take place out of time, since it is not actually time related.

Also, the very foundation of happiness, as well as real love, is Acceptance.

Unconditional love starts with acceptance, or it wouldn't be unconditional. In many regards both happiness and love are declarations, which can garner more intense feelings of love and happiness over time.

You certainly can't be happy if you are resisting "what is," in any way. So, acceptance is an important step on the road to happiness and love. It doesn't mean you don't want to do something about the current situation. It is just that by accepting it, you are not allowing the current situation to ruin your experience of being happy and loving NOW.

Coming back to the rose-colored glasses, some of the different contexts to "come from," are Being Grateful, Appreciative, and Thankful for your life.

Once you take those positions, put on those glasses, or take a stand for that reality (different ways of saying the same thing), you will start to gather evidence for that reality.

Recognize that you do the same thing with a negative outlook. You feel depressed and gather evidence for being depressed. So why not train your mind through practice, to use that ability to create a positive experience of happiness? Another example of this kind of contextual shift, which we discussed earlier, would be seeing your upsets as an opportunity, rather than a problem, therefore welcoming them as the next step on your Path to Freedom.

There is a balance here. You are not struggling with the way it is, nor are you resisting it or denying it. You are accepting it as what your current creation has brought forth.

You are looking at reality for what it is, without attachment, just seeing what is so. Now, this doesn't mean you don't have preferences or intend to do something about what is, you are just not using an experience of unhappiness and dissatisfaction to drive you to make the change.

For example, suppose you are holding yourself as a learner, willing to make mistakes and to get feedback in order to learn. You are happy as a learner, excited by the adventure and journey of life and you are open to any indication of what is required to realize your goals.

Contrast this to being defensive if you get criticized, trying always to prove that you have your act together, afraid and anxious that you will fail and be rejected. Or not going for your desires 100% because you may offend someone or fail and then reveal what a failure as a person you are! What a different reality!

In one, you are an insecure, needy person trying to get your needs met. In the other reality, you are still as incompetent as you were before, yet you embrace the incompetence as the first step of any learner becoming competent, and you are happy for the opportunity.

You can create that. It is in your power and you have not changed one aspect of the Illusionary Bubble Reality, you have only changed where you "come from" and who you are Being in this reality.

Shakespeare said, *"There is nothing either good or bad but thinking makes it so."* If you are practicing meditation, you will start to disengage your thoughts from what is happening. This ability is essential in the process of transformation.

For a moment, think about your own **Self-Talk**. Do you beat yourself up when you do less than you think you could or should? Do you hold an idea or image of perfection against which you judge yourself? Have you taken on your mother's or father's role of criticizing you? Do you sometimes feel bad, wrong, guilty, or angry at yourself, for what you have done? These experiences are all self-created and require some sense of the different levels of reality to unravel them.

For example, what you did physically is the most real -you did something that doesn't work, that did not produce the desired result. Are you willing to accept that as perhaps the starting point of a learning process or as a lesson you learned from and won't forget? Or are you letting the image in your mind of perfection be what you are holding onto as the senior reality? You have taken on the mechanism of punishing yourself as supposedly the way to learn, and look what it does to your happiness. The thought of a better way to do something may be your impetus for change yet should not be your reason for feeling guilty or beating yourself up.

This is how by being present to yourself, by being awake, you will see and then practice correcting those behaviors that rob you of the moment-by-moment experience of happiness. That is why a commitment to happiness is such a truth telling mirror to indicate that some mechanism is at play when you are not happy. My first move is always to look to see if I am accepting things the way they are or resisting them.

As you identify more and more of your experience for what it actually is through your self-inquiry and meditation practice, you will naturally expand into the constant, unchangeable Awareness that you are. That which has no form yet is aware of all forms. That which is Aware that you are Aware of your experience.

I want to emphasize, as explained earlier, that there are only a few categories of what is: physical sensations located in the general area you call, "my body," and emotions that mostly have a physical corollary, in that they are located somewhere.

Then there are the many thought forms that arise, opinions, beliefs, concepts, names, visual images, fantasies, and the succession of apparently related thoughts we call thinking.

Then there are the sensations of smell, taste, and touch, and perceptions of sight and sound. Again, take a moment to notice that the experience of seeing and hearing is out there in space where you say the object is or the sound comes from. Finally, there is the experience of the greater reality, kind of all held together by concepts, beliefs, interpretations (all thoughts), made up of all-of these forms. And that is it!

You are the Awareness that is aware of all that, without judgement (that is just another thought), or assessments as to what is good or bad, etc. You are peaceful, constant, eternal Awareness. Meditation and contemplation will help you experience this, usually in small bites.

The Illusion has such a pull, continually yanking us back into its trance, the identification with our body and our social role or persona, and the apparent reality of the changing physical world we live in. We all have to keep waking up, repeatedly. This is the Journey.

Coming from that "no place," place, that Emptiness, Consciousness, or Awareness, you will find a whole world of energy, possibility, creativity, and wisdom, and you will start to gain the freedom to exercise real choice as to what you want to create.

Exercise - Shifting Awareness
Here is a brief exercise that I learned from Craig Hamilton, in his Practice of Direct Awakening which intends to give you a direct experience of Awareness. Perhaps read through the instructions (or have someone else lead you through it), then do the exercise.

Sit comfortably with your eyes partway open and aimed down at the floor at about 45 degrees. Focus on a spot on the floor that you can rest your eyes on and throughout the following instructions, do not move your eyes to the left or right.

Now from focusing on that spot, move your awareness as far as you can to the right, in your peripheral vision. Notice what you are aware of. Now return to the center. Next move your awareness to the far left in your peripheral vision and notice what you are now aware of. Bring your awareness to center and come out of the exercise.

As you recall your experience of the exercise, did you notice that in not changing the direction of your eyes, you were able to shift awareness from right to left? As if an invisible, conscious awareness glided over to that area of what your eyes were bringing in.

The sensory perception did not change in that your eyes always registered the same view, yet your awareness roamed around. This is what the Buddhists refer to as the Emptiness, the Nothingness of Who you are, Pure Awareness.

To be complete, it is also true that the nature of everything is awareness, in that objects and awareness are intertwined and inseparable. This is why enlightened teachers say, "You are Nothing and Everything," all at the same time.

Exercise - No Head
Another fun and enlightening experiment was

introduced by a man named Douglas Harding, who woke up when he discovered experientially, that he had, "No Head."

Here are the instructions. Point your finger at an object and notice your awareness centered on the object. Notice what it feels like to be focusing on an object out there where you are pointing. Be intensely aware of "my experience of the object is entirely over there in my awareness."

Ignore the scientific explanation of seeing, that is just a thought, and do this experientially. Now take that same finger and point back to what is looking at the object. What is your experience? Isn't it just an emptiness, an aware nothingness, a presence with no form that looks out at the world of everything?

What You Truly Know

Once again, your experience confirms the only thing that you truly know right now, the only thing you know for sure and that is "I am, or I exist," not the "I," or "me," that is associated with "my," body and personality or you see looking back at you in the mirror.

As you reside more and more in this greater reality, which is always present and available, you will find yourself being more Present or more Mindful (actually more Mindless). You are HERE

NOW in a non- judgmental accepting state, more awake, more able to see the situation for what it is in all of its layers.

You can start to see the difference between your interpretation of reality and the physicality of what is happening. You can begin to distinguish how your mind brings up old patterns to distort the current situation, turns lovers into enemies, friends into adversaries and creates judgements and prejudices that push people away.

Also, since the part of you that is Aware, or who you truly are as Awareness, is whole and complete, happy, needing nothing to satisfy itself, you have a very different relationship to the present moment.

You might look into the space of what is occurring and see what is wanted and needed to create a more positive reality. You certainly will have the ability to more appropriately respond. And that makes all the difference.

I assert that a commitment to **Being Happy** is a high spiritual practice because, against the mirror of that commitment, you will see all the things you do to block that experience in your manifested self.

Think about it. Bringing happiness to others is a great contribution to them as it gives them the experience of being accepted and appreciated. And for you, you are happy, which is what you have spent your life trying to accomplish. What a win/win.

CHAPTER 8

Creating Your Future

Every human being has the inherent ability to create reality and is in fact creating reality all the time. We do it unconsciously, and then more and more consciously, as a result of waking up to who we truly are and clearing up some of the dysfunctional patterns from the past. We were all born with the same five fundamental abilities:

1. An imagination
2. An emotional guidance system
3. The ability to focus and shift our attention
4. The ability to think logically
5. The ability to take aligned actions toward a desired result.

I will discuss each in turn in an attempt to present how to use those talents in creating a positive future. First let me remind you of the trap in this conversation. You have been operating under the assumption that, "if I create this or that I will then be happy, sometime in the future." This is the great false promise of the conversation we were born into.

So, the very first premise of enlightened creation is that you have to decouple yourself from this false promise and **BE Now what you want to Become**. You must come from already being happy in this process of creation because nothing (no thing) you create can make you happy. In fact, if you believe the false promise, you are bound to end up disappointed and unhappy.

This brings us back to the BE > DO > HAVE conversation which is the metaphysical way that creation takes place. From the most etheric, idea, vision, or word, to the most physically solid, it is a process of adding more and more agreement to the idea.

I have used this example in my book, *Living Awake*, and it is a good one, so here it goes. Imagine you are an architect with the idea for a new building. There already exists a building at the site on which you intend to build. You draw up plans by translating the vision into construction details and action plans. First the foundation, then the floor, walls, etc. Right there, you have started to make it more "real" with paper, lists, and drawings.

Then you might sell the idea to an investor, so

now two of you agree on the idea (share the vision), making it a little more real. Then some more investors including the bank (a construction loan) put up the money. Most of you know that money only has value by agreement, when it is really just a piece of paper or a digital code, so the money adds more agreement.

Next you need to buy the property and demolish the old building. Does this seem like letting go of the past to make space for the new? It is.

Next the plans turn into foundations, walls, floors, a roof as many workers give their time (agreement), materials are bought and arranged in the appropriate order. Then finally the building is complete and everyone, even the doubters who didn't think it was a good idea originally, now must agree that the idea has become a reality.

Substitute what you want to create for the building in the example, becoming a board-certified doctor, or a champion athlete, or a credentialed something or other, or getting the relationship you want, or making X amount of money, or buying a house.

All these are examples of something created that was not part of your reality previously. The trap is that "I will be happier when I get those things, or I become that thing and get recognized for the accomplishment."

Do you see how strong the pull is in your own

mind? I will be accepted or admired or feel secure or feel free or feel fulfilled; I WILL BE HAPPY WHEN… For me it was for a long time, "when I get enlightened," as if enlightenment was as goal to achieve, a state to get to.

What makes these accomplishments a struggle is driven by your trying to overcome the very core of your ego, that, "I am Separate and Not OK, undeserving, inadequate, flawed, etc." The attempt to "overcome," these inadequacies actually reinforces these core beliefs about yourself, as they define "Who you are Being," in the creation process.

You have set up your own barriers to having what you want. "I want this, but I don't deserve to have what I want." With lots of struggle and effort, from time to time, people do create the desired outcome. What was the price paid in unhappiness, struggle, stress, and effort along the way?

You begin to sense that the stuff you Have or the accomplishments you Have are just hollow symbols of what you wanted and didn't get by having them – the sense of Being complete, whole, satisfied, happy and fulfilled.

A friend of mine, Stewart Emery used to say, "You never get enough of what you don't really want." You never get enough of the symbols of success (outside validation), to produce the inner experience of self- esteem and fulfillment you long for.

The Truth is that <u>you are already that which you want</u>: fulfilled, connected to everything and everyone, happy, and joyous! You, and all of us, made a big mistake when we agreed to and declared that we were Separate and Not OK. This mistake has been running (and ruining) our lives and is the source of so much suffering. What a cosmic joke we have been playing on ourselves!

In the creative process of desiring and manifesting reality, it is important to not get sucked into the Illusion's trap. The following suggestions should be helpful.

When we were looking at the process of clearing up the past, there were four steps in that process: Recognize, Take Responsibility, Discover the nature of the pattern and your ego, and "Let it go, or Let it be," and "Forgive yourself and others." These are the first four steps of the complete seven-step process of transformation.

In following these four steps, you are clearing the space for what you want to create, like tearing down the old building. You have gotten to neutral. You have returned to some degree of being aware of being aware, your true self, the aware presence.

Now you can do consciously what you did as a

child unconsciously. You have always been a creative force. In the past, this creative force was used to reinforce your insecurities, by trying to overcome them or hide them, both being forms of resistance or denial.

This includes reinforcing the reality of your limitations, your limiting beliefs. From a neutral stance, you can now return to the childlike state of wonder and being a learner in the creative process.

The next three steps of the seven-step process of transformation are:

- Declare Anew
- Practice and Get Feedback
- Wisdom/Mastery

Declare Anew

Out of the aware emptiness that you are, you declare a new way of Being, a new way of Showing Up. As an example, suppose you used to judge and put other people down. Now you see that behavior for what it was: a way of making yourself better than others in an attempt to enhance your ego and overcome your insecurity of worthlessness.

You now declare yourself supportive of others, cooperative, and a good listener. This is a stand you take, even if there is little or no evidence to support the reality of this new way of Being. It comes out of nothing.

This next point is important. Keep imagining your vision of the future until you can feel what it would be like to Be that way in life, to experience the satisfaction, the sense of self-esteem, the enhanced feeling of loving yourself. This vibrational state is what will attract, draw towards you, the vision you are creating.

This is where your natural ability of having an imagination comes in. Imagine Being that way, acting out of that way of Being in what you Do and say. Feel what it is like as others start responding to you from this new way, rather than the old ego pattern of righteousness, defensiveness and judgement.

All five natural abilities are needed in the creative process. Imagine and declare who you are now considering yourself to Be, your new role in life. Check to see that your emotional guidance system gives a green light because you feel good about yourself, happy that you are on a path of your own choosing. If your emotions don't confirm your choice, go back to the drawing board. You have got to feel good about who you are Being and what you are Doing, which is the aligned action part. And coming up with your plan of action requires some focused thinking.

Core Values
It is a good idea at this point of creating a new way of

showing up in the world, to make sure you are clear about your core values. Acting in accordance with your core values (right action in the Buddhist tradition) will create an internally generated experience of self-esteem which is not dependent on any form of outside validation from others. These core values become the very core of your new personality and they must be maintained by you, for you.

Some examples of core values:

- I am honest. I tell the truth to myself and others
- I am authentic, what you see is what I am
- I am loving
- I am a good person who wants to contribute to others and our world
- I am willing to be responsible at all times
- I am generous.

Spend some time identifying your core values as they will become the very foundation of who you consider your new Self to Be and the basis of your experience of Integrity.

Recall a time when you did something you felt was wrong or out of integrity or a betrayal of your values. How did you feel about yourself? Bad, low self-worth, low self-esteem. You must be responsible for maintaining your own self esteem by living in accordance with your core values. And positive self-esteem is the absolute necessary foundation for creating a positive reality.

As a young adult, I once went into a store and switched prices on an item so that I paid a lesser price. I was so upset with myself that the next day I returned to the store, apologized, and paid the difference. I just wasn't willing to live with myself doing something I did not feel good about. And I realized that I was in control of how I felt about myself.

I have remembered that valuable learning experience whenever I might be tempted in the future. We all have to live with ourselves. As we gain consciousness, we become more and more the product of our own creation and in so doing generate the self-love we all long for. This living in accordance with your core values is what **Integrity** is all about. Being whole, complete, authentic and transparent.

Staying Focused

Maintain as much **focused attention** as you can on what you are creating: your new way of Being and your Desired Vision. This commitment, or stand, you have made, acts as a mirror to see what gets in your way.

This is not some new idea, as Buddha is reported to have said some 2500 years ago:

"What you think you become,
What you feel you attract,
What you imagine you create."

Look for what slows the process down or actually stops you. Often it is that you are distracted by the current reality or the plethora of things you might be interested in, that take your attention away from what you are creating. Try turning off the television or stop reading the news for a few days. See what happens. Experiment.

Esther and Jerry Hicks, authors of, *The Law of Attraction*, say, *"like attracts like."* You attract that which is in harmonic resonance with who you are Being and the beliefs you hold. Do you notice beliefs that don't allow the new reality to come to you? Like a belief "that I can't do this, or this isn't me, or people won't like me if I speak out."

When you see these beliefs, let them go and declare beliefs that are more in alignment with your new way of being. For example, "there is a lot of evidence that the world is cooperative and not just competitive (survival of the fittest) and people will respond to me favorably when I cooperate."

Or "when I am not trying to be better than others, people will want to hear my view, which is my unique expression in the world." "I live in a world of sufficiency, not scarcity."

Remember that we are not only creating who we are in the world but also our version of the world itself. Creation starts with a declaration, then we take aligned actions consistent with the declaration and gather the evidence that agrees with the declaration. This reinforces the declaration and makes it more and more "real" in the Illusionary game we all live in.

There is another aspect to consider as you DO actions <u>that are aligned</u> with your new declaration and BE your new way of showing up in the world. You have already created an agreement field around your old way of Being. You have been in an "agreed upon," dance with others.

Here is where you could even take responsibility for having entrained others around you on how to be with you or your having attracted people who fit, in a co- dependent way, with your patterns. It may take some time to gradually change that agreement reality and others may be somewhat surprised and upset when you change the game on them. So be understanding, compassionate and patient. And you may actually be surprised at how quickly things do turn around.

It is a totally different experience to be "<u>in</u> the world, not <u>of</u> the world." Playing the game consciously rather than acting out of your worldly conditioning and patterns.

Practice & Feedback

Practice and receiving **Feedback** is how you learned as a child. Since you are now not trying to prove you are OK and are willing to accept and admit that you have failings and insecurities, just like every other human being, you can once again return to that wondrous state of Being a Learner. You are <u>OK with being Not OK.</u> Isn't that a relief?

Being a Learner will allow you to be open to receiving and even asking for feedback. As you go through this learning process, notice the tendency of your mind to be distracted and to start focusing on other things. It might distract you with your current problems. We all tend to get drawn into the reality of what is occurring. Or we get sucked into what others complain about, or letting the nightly news draw our attention away.

You need to focus on what you are creating, not your current reality. Your thoughts follow your focus and your actions come out of your thoughts, so keep reminding yourself of what you are creating, your new intention to BE a certain way and the new reality you are creating.

Perhaps a morning ritual of restating who you consider yourself to be, or a note on the bathroom mirror that says, "I am ...," I have an example of this in my own life when I was younger, yet, I didn't get the lesson until much later in life. During my time at Yale, I was on the varsity football team, both as a sophomore, then as a junior, I was always trying to prove myself, so I would be put in the starting lineup.

I was always nervous. I tried to never make any mistakes and while I did well, it was a struggle and there was always the anxiety of "would I make it this week?" I had a few starts, I mostly played second string.

Here is where it changed. Senior year I thought, "I am the best tight end Yale has this year" and my whole attitude changed. I asked for feedback and correction. I had fun. I was still nervous about the games, however I felt secure, fulfilled and appreciated – all the things I wanted to feel from having, "made it."

As it turned out, I received the "Lineman of the Year," award and several professional offers, which I am happy I did not take up. The point is that during that year, I started by Being a success, even though I did not have the evidence for it yet. And I was willing to ask for coaching and feedback, which made me into a better player, which ultimately produced the results I had.

Later, when I was 48, I took up rowing and thoroughly enjoyed the process of becoming a national and international masters champion. I was always looking for how to improve my stroke, my conditioning, and my race strategy.

It has been a joy to be a learner of this sport over the last 30 years. Now I can say, to some extent, I have mastered the stroke. It is natural to me when I get in a boat. I don't have to think about it and I am able to contribute my entrained wisdom (what I know is now experienced in my body) to others as a coach. I simply share my experience of how I do the stroke. It is kind of like driving a car without the struggle and concentration it took to learn how to drive. Now I am able to think about other stuff while driving, and not even remembering the journey, yet driving aware, conscious, and alert for any potential problems.

Being a Learner

As a learner you will go through several steps in **the learning process**. And the question is, "Are you willing to be happy, being a learner?" Learning to drive a car is a good example, as most of us have gone through that learning process.

Now as an adult, can you be humble enough and authentic enough to just BE where you are in the learning process? If you have done the work as you have read through this handbook and are now able to let go of your needing to prove yourself and hide your insecurities and incompetencies, it should be easy, a walk in the park.

Four Stages of Competency

Unconscious Incompetence
You start with **unconscious incompetence.** You don't know what you don't know. At this stage, to continue the analogy of driving, your parents better not let you behind the wheel! It is a good idea to admit that this is where you are, if it is true. "I am a rank beginner in this domain."

Conscious Incompetence
Next you move to **conscious incompetence.** You start the learning process, by first, intellectually learning about the subject, where is everything and how it works. You read the book. Then perhaps with a teacher, mentor or coach, you begin practicing, getting feedback, and correcting.

Conscious Competence
Eventually you arrive at **conscious competence** where you still have to pay attention to do it skillfully.

Unconscious/ "Transparent" Competence
Finally, you move to what is called **unconscious (not really unconscious) "transparent," competence** where it is just the way you are. It takes no additional attention. Some people say that this is when you intuitively know what to do. This is what Wisdom/Mastery is.

From Wisdom/Mastery, you can contribute to others by sharing your learning process. You are "walking the talk," and being an inspirational example of that possibility for others.

Happily Creating

Besides visualizing and focusing on what you want to create, which initiates the creative process, you need to BE who you want to Become. This vibration of who you are Being will attract to you what you desire. It is the only way you create your own happiness in every moment of now, while you are gaining the skills, competencies, and accomplishments that are the manifestation of your desires.

You see, BE>DO>HAVE are all happening at once, in the NOW. You are Being who you want to Become. You are Doing whatever is the next aligned action step towards your goal, and you are Having the experience of manifesting (through time) a result, which in the end is just one of many milestones on a lifelong journey.

Many people believe that "the Ends justifies the Means," and that only creates suffering, unhappiness, struggle and disappointment along the way.

You will discover that there is Only the Journey and it is your job to **BE HAPPY** on it. This is the highest spiritual discipline.

Assignment

In your journal create a vision for what you desire in each of the domains you have identified. Then define who you are Being that is consistent and appropriate to that vision. Then on some timely basis, like weekly or monthly, review your vision and identify actions that are aligned with your vision and who you have declared yourself as Being.

Then get into action. You have to get into action to be in the game. This will give you results (feedback) that you can use to correct or learn from.

CHAPTER 9

Transformation in Action:

Applying What You Have Learned to a Typical Day

You get up early and are not too enthusiastic about the day - nothing really exciting to look forward to. Your mind goes back and forth, "should I or shouldn't I work out?" Since you are committed to being happy you think, "Perhaps I could work out and not push it so hard, or perhaps I will listen to a podcast I am interested in while I ride the stationary bike. I know I will feel better physically if I work out." So, off to the gym you go.

You are surrendering to what you are committed to, being physically active, healthy and in shape and you are finding ways to make it enjoyable.

You come back home, have breakfast with the children, pack their lunches and send them off to school. Yes, it is routine, and you realize that these years with them as children will soon pass and you experience a moment of gratitude for them and your life, realizing that Acceptance for "the way things are," is the foundation for happiness and love (even when it seems challenging).

Your spouse has left for work in a rush, leaving dirty dishes in the sink and dish towels not hung up. You notice yourself start to get annoyed and judge your spouse as being inconsiderate. You feel hurt and unappreciated. In that moment, turning the person you love into an enemy. You write a note reminding yourself to bring it up when the two of you talk in the evening, so you won't hold any resentment all day long. You also recognize that you are judging him or her against an ideal standard and making him/her wrong for not complying. All insights to be shared later.

Off to work you go experiencing a bit of anxiety about what might come up at the office. As you drive, you acknowledge that your intentions are positive and you will do the best you can, perhaps learning something along the way, and you need to let things occur as they do.

Then if the situation doesn't meet what you think is possible, you will have a real starting point for putting in corrective action. No need to be upset. In fact, you realize that if you get upset, it will only distort your decision- making process.

If what is happening at the office is a recurring upset, like "I don't experience being listened to or valued or I feel criticized and invalidated," you will set aside some time later to do a discovery process on this recurring upset.

During your noon break, you take 15 minutes to meditate and disconnect from your thoughts. For these 15 minutes you will do nothing except sit quietly and practice coming into the present moment. You reinforce the experience that who you truly are is the Conscious Awareness that is aware of all aspects of your life experience.

In the afternoon, you practice some of the intentions you are working on as a manager: Acknowledging others more, asking questions and becoming a better listener, seeking ways to support your team being more satisfied, efficient and productive.

After dinner with your children and spouse when everyone had a chance to share about their day, you set aside a half hour to do the discovery process on the recurring upset from that morning.

Then you and your spouse share about what you have seen that sabotages your experience of love and connection. This is when you bring up the dirty dishes and how it triggered your feelings of being taken for granted and not valued. You take full responsibility for your experience - no blaming. You then ask what was going on with your spouse - you are curious. Perhaps you make some agreements about the future, the upset feels resolved.

Before you go to sleep you snuggle and say what each of you are grateful for and several things you can acknowledge your partner for. You end with "I love you," before you go to sleep.

A good day in your life. You have done your best and learned what you could. You feel happy to be alive and on life's journey.

IN CLOSING

I want to welcome you to the lifelong process of transformation. You have the tools for success. It is now up to you to put them into practice.

While I was finishing this book, there was a day in which I had nothing I was looking forward to, nothing planned. I was not experiencing being very happy (and yet I was writing this book on happiness!) and there seemed to be no real reason to be unhappy. I noticed my energy was down and I was withdrawing into myself. My wife, Diane, noticed it and said something about not feeling connected. I kept looking and realized that I had a deep seated, underlying anger that, "life was not giving me what I wanted," kind of like a fundamental rage that "this can't be it," the ultimate victim of life.

By sitting with that experience, a little more, images of being born started to surface, the slap on the small of my back, crying out, being cold, rough cloth on my skin, taken away from my mother, and the whole notion that "this isn't what I expected it to be like." Something like, I was happy with high expectations for a good time coming into this human birth and then being severely disappointed.

I realized that from the level of who I truly am, I was happy that I got in touch with this very basic pattern that has played out throughout my life. That in my commitment to my own evolution, this is the Path. That only by it showing up in my experience could I get in touch with the pattern, even though for a short while it affected my mood and my connection with Diane. By my seeing it for what it is, and by Diane and I talking about it, we were able to let it go, see the perfection of the process and recommit to our on-going transformation.

I share this so you are abundantly clear that I too am a fellow traveler on this transformational journey.

Remember, enlightenment is not a stance or an experience to get to, it is an experience to come from. Transformation is the ongoing process of waking up to deeper and deeper aspects of this Illusionary Reality we find ourselves in.

Your true self is enlightened already. Whole, complete, loving and happy, all the qualities you would ever aspire to. Now it is your job to let go of what is blocking those qualities from manifesting. So go for it, let your light shine forth.

If there is anything I can do to support you in evolving along this path, please contact me through:

Website: "**LandonCarter.com**"

Email: "**landon@landoncarter.co.nz**"

All the very best,

Landon

Recommended Reading:

Eckhart Tolle (1999)
The Power of Now.
New World Library

Eckhart Tolle (2005)
A New Earth: Awakening to Your Life's Purpose.
Namaste Publishing

Michael A. Singer (2007)
The Untethered Soul: The Journey Beyond Yourself.
New Harbinger Publications

Michael A. Singer (2022)
Living Untethered: Beyond the Human Predicament.
New Harbinger Publications

Esther and Jerry Hicks (2006)
The Law of Attraction: The Basics of the Teachings of Abraham.
Hay House

Rupert Spira (2017)
Being Aware of Being Aware.
Sahaja Publications

Rubert Spira (2022)
You Are the Happiness You Seek:
Uncovering the Awareness of Being
Sahaja Publications

Landon Carter (2013)
Living Awake: The Practice of Transforming
Everyday Life.
Carter Covington Publishing

Landon Carter (2014)
The Awakened Relationship: Transforming Upsets
and Blame Into Love and Harmony.
Marshall & McClintic Publishing

Diane Covington Carter & Landon Carter (2013)
Falling in Love Backwards: An Unlikely Tale of
Happily Ever After.
Marshall & McClintic Publishing

Recommended Courses/Workshops

The Practice of Direct Awakening
A 12-week online meditation course
Go to: craighamiltonglobal.com

The Landmark Forum
Go to: Landmarkworldwide.com

Triton Leadership
Go to: Tritonleadershipcoaching.com

Acknowledgements

This book is the result of 50 years of experience on the spiritual/human potential path, so it is difficult to remember all who have contributed to my insights and understandings. There have been numerous books, starting with Paramahansa Yogananda's landmark book, <u>Autobiography of a Yogi</u>.

I have listed the most current books that reinforce what I have written about in my recommended reading list, but there were many more over the years, too many to name. To all of those authors, I acknowledge their desire to contribute to a happier, better world and I thank them for what I learned.

To Werner Erhard, thank you for your contribution to me and for your training in the realm of transformation.

To John Hanley Jr., thank you for inviting me to partner in online trainings during the recent pandemic. I have thoroughly enjoyed working with you who understands this material and has such a deep commitment to transforming people's lives in a meaningful way.

A huge thank you to Steve Pomerance, Michelle Yacoel, Erinn Hayes, Andrew Simon PhD., Dr. Shira Bush, Jason Danielson, Lynne Twist, and Joel and Judy Kimmel for reading drafts of this book and giving me feedback. I so appreciate your support and commitment to having this book contribute to the happiness of others.

I could not have completed this book without the layout work of Margie Baxley and the book cover by Susan Whiting. Thank you both.

I wish to thank my wife, Diane, for her continued support and help. As an author herself and teacher of writing, she has edited many drafts, given me feedback on how to express ideas and much appreciated encouragement to take the next step in the publishing process.

Finally, I wish to thank you, the reader. If you have gotten this far, it is a validation of your intention to have your life be all that is possible. And the more you come from being whole, complete and happy, from your true Self, the better choices you will make and the better world we will all be creating. So thank you for being a part of the team.

Made in United States
Troutdale, OR
04/04/2024

18937610R00100